FIBERARTS DESIGN BOOK SIX

Edited by
Nancy Orban

FIBERARTS DESIGN BOOK SIX

Edited by
Nancy Orban

LARK BOOKS
Asheville, North Carolina

VALUABLE ASSISTANCE

Dawn Cusick

Jackie Flenner

Kathleen Holmes

Rosemary Kast

Susan Kieffer

Megan Kirby

Celia Naranjo

Jean Wall Penland

Rob Pulleyn

Chris Rich

Melissa Stanz

Nicole Tuggle

Cover: Astrid Hilger Bennett. India Cafe (detail).

Editor   Nancy Orban
Art Director   Celia Naranjo
Art Assistant   Hannes Charen

10 9 8 7 6 5 4 3 2 1

First Edition

Published by Lark Books
50 College Street
Asheville, North Carolina 28801, USA

© 1999 Lark Books

For information about distribution in the U.S., Canada, the U.K., Europe, and Asia,
call Lark Books at 828-253-0467.

Distributed in Australia by Capricorn Link (Australia) Pty Ltd.,
P.O. Box 6651, Baulkham Hills Business Centre, NSW 2153, Australia

Distributed in New Zealand by Southern Publishers Group,
22 Burleigh St., Grafton, Auckland, New Zealand

Distributed in South Africa by Phambili Agencies cc, P.O. Box 28680,
Kensington 2101, Johannesburg, South Africa

Printed in Hong Kong

ISSN: 1524-2935
ISBN 1-57990-126-3

CONTENTS

FOREWORD

Before we wrote this introduction, we thought it would be appropriate to wander through the previous five *Fiberarts Design Books* in order to get some perspective on this constantly evolving field we call "fiber."

The term fiber has always been somewhat amorphous and inclusive; it covers a variety of techniques—stitchery, needlework, basketry, weaving, surface design (using dyes), quilting, clothing, and felting—all of which have in common the use of fabric, thread, yarn, dye, or reed. We first used the term when we started *Fiberarts Magazine* in the mid-1970s.

The first time a *Fiberarts Design Book* was published 20 years ago was the first time that artists and craftspeople who worked in these fields shared a common showcase. The book was, as it is now, open to both professional artists whose works are displayed in major museums and to amateurs who are driven to create without thought of professional careers. The judging has always been anonymous.

To organize the work we wanted to exhibit in that initial *Design Book*, we cleverly came up with chapter headings that reflected the various techniques included in the term "fiber," and most of the work we featured fit comfortably into those categories. The weavers wove, the quilters quilted, and the stitchers stitched. Neat, orderly, predictable. There were, of course, a few errant artists whose work didn't fit comfortably into a particular category, so we conveniently came up with a chapter called "Diversions."

Flash forward to this volume—the sixth.

Although we've maintained most of the chapter headings that we've used in the past, they're less and less meaningful, in part because today's fiber work isn't easily divided into categories. Perhaps only tapestry weavers still focus on maintaining a strict definition of their craft. For almost everyone else, the definition of what constitutes, for example, a quilt or a basket, is as vague and arguable as what constitutes art itself.

Our task this time was made even more complex by the large number of works that combine two or more techniques. Artists in fiber have always felt free to borrow techniques from their colleagues. The definition of colleague, however, has expanded to include not only other fiber artists, but artists in general. We faced some challenging decisions: Is a painted fabric panel a quilt or a painting? Is a computer-generated work computer art or a weaving?

These questions certainly make it difficult for anyone who has to categorize fiber art work, but so what? The very fact that contemporary fiber work is usually an amalgam of techniques and materials is what makes it so interesting, so alive, and so important. To distort a familiar 1960s aphorism, contemporary artists now ask which mediums are appropriate for what they want to say, rather than letting particular mediums define their messages. This evolutionary process has stretched over the past two decades, of course; comparing the first *Design Book* with the one we're introducing now makes it an easy process to see.

Making distinctions between the fiber art in this volume and the fiber art in the last one isn't easy. Evolution is hard to define when you're only studying a four-year-long period. But that won't stop us from making a few observations.

We've noticed a greater use of representational imagery. We're intrigued, for example, by the increase in use of the image of the hand, the image of the human body (frequently nude), and architecture (both grand and domestic). We've also noticed, not surprisingly, more dependence on the computer for the design and/or execution of work and, conversely, more hand-embroidered work. Surface designers are embellishing their work with beading, embroidery, and stitching; basketmakers seem to have moved on to other techniques. Clothing makers either seem to be focusing on beautiful fabric and simple silhouettes or abandoning all restraint and going for the outrageous. More fiber artists are including humor in their work—a change we applaud—and are maintaining their fascination with the letter, the word, and the phrase. And we notice that more work is self referential, telling stories and sharing "pictures" of the artist's youth, family, body, and idiosyncracies.

Twenty years ago, there was little communication between fiber artists. The stitchers talked with stitchers, the papermakers met with papermakers. Over the last two decades, artists have been talking to, sharing with, and teaching each other more and more. The results of these conversations are documented in this book.

Increasingly, these conversations have also been between artists from various cultural backgrounds. The few thousand entrants to the first *Design Book* were almost exclusively from North America. For this book, we received 5,500 entries from a total of 36 countries. We used to be able to tell whether or not a work was from North America just by looking at it, but that's almost impossible today.

Although we've maintained the same vague criteria for judging works into the book (artistic prowess, technical acumen, and "I don't know why, but I really want that piece in the book"), the process is more and more difficult—and wonderful. Our goal has always been to produce a book that accurately represents the diversity, artistic integrity, unique vision, and sheer joy that comprise the fiber arts. In 20 years, we'll probably be able to do a better job of analyzing the fiber art in this volume, but we can't wait that long to share these works with you. Welcome to *Fiberarts Design Book Six*. Enjoy!

The FIBERARTS Staff

NEEDLEWORK

ELAINE McBRIDE
UNITED STATES

Aunt Bernice Was Miss Gulch!
Embroidery; cotton floss on muslin; 6½ by 5¾ in.

A

COLLEEN O'ROURKE
UNITED STATES

Rooftop

Embroidery; seed beads; 14 by 18 in. Photo: Thomas H. O'Rourke

This piece was inspired by a party I attended in Chicago. It struck me as a uniquely urban scene, especially when the "El" train flew by every 20-or-so minutes.

B

OLGA DVIGOUBSKY CINNAMON
UNITED STATES

Into the Light of Day

Crochet, beadwork; waxed linen, metallic thread, glass beads; 12½ by 4½ by 1½ in. Photo: Jeff Owen

Like the earth, people have "light" and "dark" moods, and the hue in between allows us to reinvent ourselves.

C

ROB WATT
UNITED STATES

Portrait

Embroidery; cotton thread on silk; 8½ by 7 in.

This is based on an oil portrait of my grandmother, although it did not have the masks and she was not as colorfully dressed.

D

GWENDOLYN L. KELLY
UNITED STATES

Comfort Zone

Embroidery, etching, collage; hand-printed fabric; 18 by 14 in.

E

JULIANNA MAHLEY
UNITED STATES

Eyeno

Embroidery; cotton; 6 by 6 in.

F

CONNIE LEHMAN
UNITED STATES

night visit, violeta

Russian needlepunch, embroidery; glass beads, lapis lazuli, pearls, sequins, silk; 5½ by 6⅝ in.

G

LORE EDZARD
UNITED STATES

Carneval I

Embroidery; cotton, rayon, silk, metallic thread; 10½ by 9½ in.

A

B

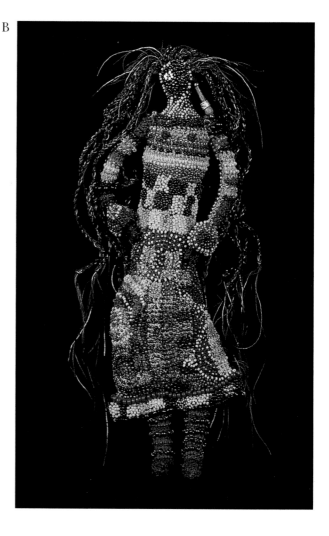

C

E

F

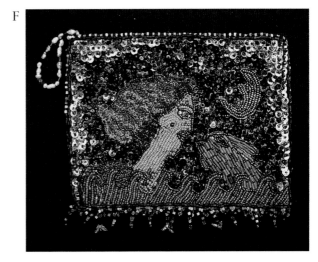

D

G

A

Family Ties

B

C

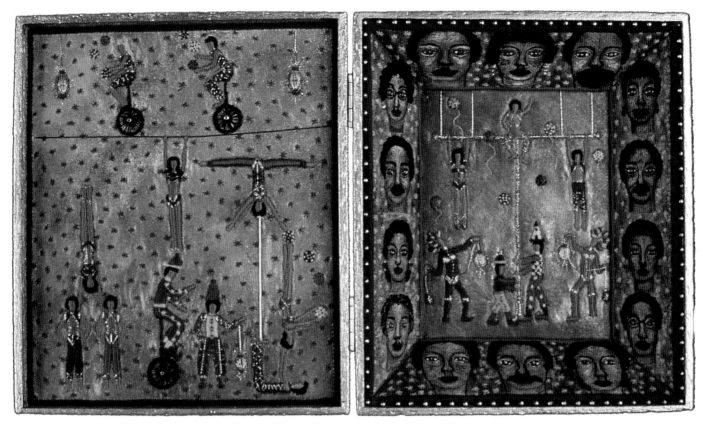

D

E

A

CINDY HICKOK
UNITED STATES

Family Ties
Machine embroidery; rayon;
6 by 6 in. Photo: Maria Davila

B

MISSY STEVENS
UNITED STATES

My Home, My Home
Loop pile embroidery; silk, cotton,
rayon, glass beads; 7 by 5¼ in.
Photo: William B. Seitz

*My thread paintings are done in a
loop-pile technique that is
worked with the smallest punch
needle. Because they are so small,
the viewer is drawn to the piece.
This intimacy of close viewing is
akin to the distance of friends in
conversation—close enough to
see expression but not so close
that you can't see each other's
entire face.*

C

ROSITA JOHANSON
CANADA

Cirque Du Soleil (detail)
Hand and machine embroidery;
cotton and metallic thread, beads,
wood, metal leaf; 6½ by 11 by 1¾
in. Photo: Lenscape Incorporated

D

CAROL BURNS
UNITED STATES

Un Mio Ritratto
Hand stitching; sequins, beads;
37 by 37 in.

*The imagery (a self portrait)
relates to the allegorical associations of a verse from Dante's
Divine Comedy in which the dark
forest symbolizes the struggle to
find one's way in life.*

E

MARY BERO
UNITED STATES

Self-Portrait: Black & White
Embroidery, couching, knotting;
cotton, silk; 7¼ by 6⅛ in. Photo:
Jim Wildeman/Wildeman Photographics

*Black/white; ying/yang; rich/poor;
good/evil*

F

AMY ORR
UNITED STATES

Three Row Houses
Beading, stitching, assembling;
velvet, steel, plastic; 16 by 36 in.
Photo: John Woodin

F

A

ELAINE MCBRIDE
UNITED STATES

Slow Cooker Triptych
Embroidery; cotton floss on muslin; 6¼ by 6 in.

I explore vestiges of my past and present. The slow, methodical approach of embroidery is an important aspect as I contemplate the images while they are stitched.

B

MARY BERO
UNITED STATES

Stuffed Head: Potentiality
Embroidery, knotting, stuffing; silk, textile ink; 5⅝ by 3¾ by ½ in. Photo: Jim Wildeman/Wildeman Photographics

C

JOHN HAWTHORNE
UNITED STATES

The Grand Illusion
Embroidery, beading; linen, cotton, metallic thread, beads; 20½ by 14 in.

D

DIANE FITZGERALD, VALORIE HARLOW, BARB MCLEAN
UNITED STATES

The Three Furies: Megaera, Tisiphone and Alecto
Applied and peyote stitch beadwork; glass and seed beads, found objects; each piece 15 by 30 by 10 in.

Left to right are Alecto, Unceasing Rage by V. Harlow, Tisiphone, Avenger of Murder by D. Fitzgerald, and Megaera, The Jealous One by B. McLean.

E

SALLEY MAVOR
UNITED STATES

On Halloween
Embroidery, fabric relief, wrapping, dyeing; velveteen, silk, felt, artificial leaves; 16 by 22 by 1 in. Photo: Tom Kleindinst, reprinted by permission of Orchard Books

A

C

B

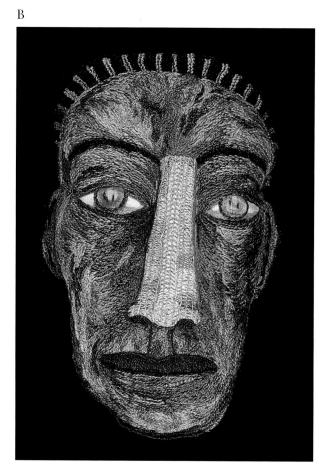

D

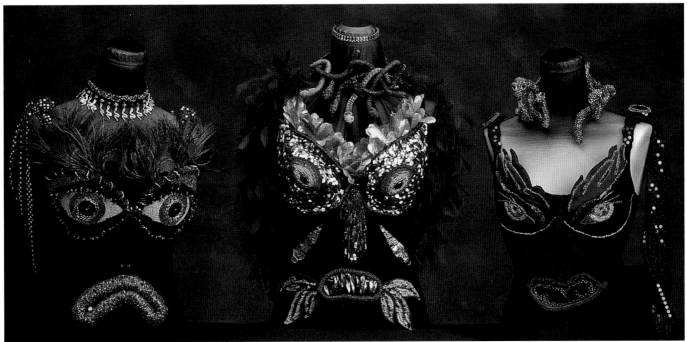

E

On Halloween...

A

CAROL ANN SMITH
ENGLAND

Basilica
Hand and machine embroidery,
applique, dyeing, painting; organ-
zas, rayon; 24 by 24 in.

B

JEAN LITTLEJOHN
ENGLAND

Echoes, New Zealand
Hand and machine stitching,
applique; linen, paper, silk,
acrylic paints; 40 by 54 in.
Photo: Michael Wicks

A

B

C

D

C

DONNA DURBIN
UNITED STATES

Flora #5

Stitching, surface design, mixed-media tapestry, stamping, collage; coffee bean bags, fabrics, raffia, yarn; 26 by 26 in.

Giving new life by transforming bits and pieces of cloth into a visual form is a process of trusting my creative intuition.

D

SUSAN FINER
UNITED STATES

Sensitive Creatures

Embroidery; perle cotton on cotton, wood, metal, and glass beads, buttons; 20 by 26 in.
Photo: Hemenway and Skrivanek

E

NANCY LEE-WRAGG
ENGLAND

Pots With Spirals

Free machine embroidery, felting; hand-dyed merino wool, silk; 8½ by 4¾ in.

Dyeing wool and silk, and hand felting, allow me to construct my own "canvas" on which to stitch and draw. I enjoy the qualities of felt and the way it can distort, grow, spread, or become three dimensional.

E

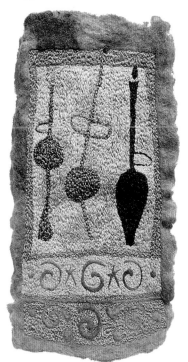

A

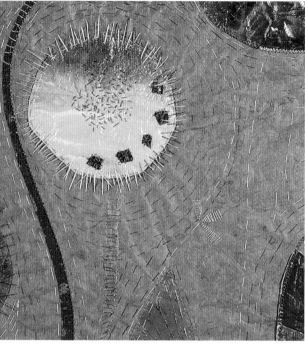

A

VALERIE JEFFRIES
ENGLAND

*The Cat, The Bird,
and The Tree* *(and detail)*
Applique, stitchery; handmade
paper, tissue paper; 58 by 38 in.

*Ancient paintings and textiles
from Asia and the Middle East
often depict images relating to
religion, myth, and everyday life.
They appear exotic and sometimes magical as they embrace
color and the decorative in a
way that is curious and seems
strange to our Western culture.*

B

JAN BEANEY
ENGLAND

Journey to Wanaka
Machine and hand embroidery;
39 by 30 in. Photo: Michael
Wicks

*This panel celebrates a wonderful
visit to New Zealand.*

C

C

RENIE BRESKIN ADAMS
UNITED STATES

Spot of Sky
Embroidery; cotton fabric and
thread; 5⅛ by 6½ in.

*I love still life paintings that cele-
brate our daily rituals, and was
thinking of Paul Cezanne when I
did this.*

D

JACQUELINE GOVIN
FRANCE

Quiet Life
Applique, embroidery, dyeing,
painting; silk, cotton, ribbons;
13 by 9½ in. Photo: Jacqueline
Hyde

E

MORAG GILBART
ENGLAND

Knave of Hearts
Machine and hand embroidery,
applique; wool, silk, cotton; 22
by 17 in.

D

E

A

ANNA TORMA
CANADA

Lullaby III
Embroidery, stitching; cotton,
wool, linen; 78½ by 51 in.

*This work contains some child-
hood memories of Hungary.*

B

JACQUES SAINT-MARTIN
FRANCE

Untitled No. 1
Embroidery; cotton thread on
linen; 11½ by 14¼ in.

C

HELEN BANZHAF
ENGLAND

Untitled
Free machine embroidery;
cotton; 11½ by 7¾ in.
Photo: Jacqui Hurst

D

PEGGY LOVE
UNITED STATES

Joy
Embroidery; linen, cotton;
8½ by 8½ by 1 in.

E

PASCALE GOLDENBERG
GERMANY

The Door
Machine piecing and embroidery; commercial fabrics;
10 by 7 in.

F

SUSAN TABER AVILA
UNITED STATES

Bolsa de Valores
Machine stitching, construction;
recycled fabric, thread; 46 by 22
by 4 in. Photo: Jacques Cressaty

*Some of the wrapped fabric balls
are held tenuously in place while
others are allowed to float freely.
The title plays on the idea of the
stock market as an unstable form
but can be translated literally as
"a bag of good things," which
presents an optimistic view of
chance.*

A

B

C

D

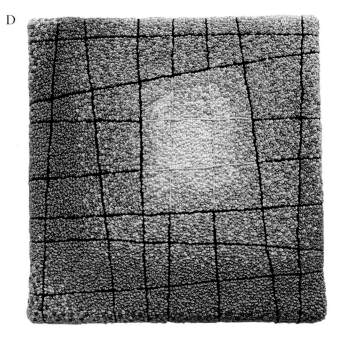

E

F

A

Chris Allen-Wickler
UNITED STATES

Listener

Peyote stitch; beads, river rock;
7 by 5½ by 4 in. Photo: Peter Lee

*Listener is from the "Visible
Soul" series, which stems from
the simultaneous loss of my
mother and the birth of my children. I use stone as a metaphor
for the soul. The surface of the
stone is composed of elements
that parallel our own delicate
skin. The labor intensive process
of stitching beads is a way of
making a mark, and it becomes a
remnant of the passing of time, a
memory of breath, a record of
pulse, and an accumulation of
wisdom.*

C

Natacha Wolters
GERMANY

Precious Poetry *(and detail)*
Embroidery, band weaving; vintage silk, antique glass and metal
beads; 17 by 12 in.
Photo: Christof Wolters

*The Department for Precious
Books of the French National
Library invited me to participate
in an exhibition of embroidered
book covers. Les Odes de Sapho
was illustrated by my
painter/grandfather, Georges
Baudin in 1920.*

B

Sonya Clark
UNITED STATES

Ras Blue

Peyote stitch, embroidery; glass
beads, suede; 5 by 9 by 9 in.
Photo: Jim Nedresky

A

B

C

D

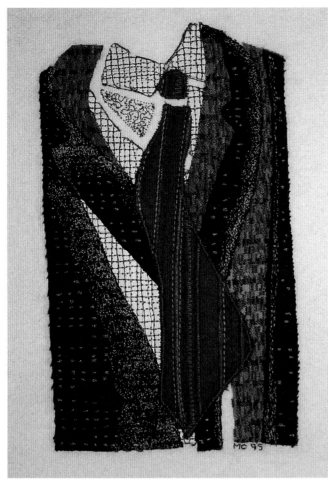

E

F

D

Margaret Charlton
ENGLAND

Red Tie
Applique, machine embroidery;
recycled shirt, jacket and tie; 8 by
5 in.

E

Richard Daehnert
UNITED STATES

Beach Relic Offering I
Machine stitching, drawing;
thread, canvas; 17¼ by 12⅜ in.
Photo: Motophoto

F

Mary Ruth Smith
UNITED STATES

Celebration
Embroidery; commercial fabric;
10 by 10 in.

A

Laura Goldberg
UNITED STATES

Birdbag

Peyote stitch; seed and embellishment beads, antique Bakelite clasp; 8 by 6 in.

B

Linda H. Konya
UNITED STATES

Self Portrait: "She's just a friend" vs. the good Navy wife

Random cross stitching; cotton, silk, linen, glass beads, mirrors; 11 by 9 in.

This piece was done after concluding a long, sad life experience. My three sons, a sense of humor, stitching, and faith brought me through.

C

Joh Ricci
UNITED STATES

Self-Portrait #1 - Chakra

Gourd stitch; seed beads, semi-precious stones, charms, sterling silver; 7¼ by 2¾ in.

A

C

B

D

E

F

D

PAMELA HASTINGS
UNITED STATES

Queen of the May Ignores Her Darker Self

Piecing, quilting, beading, soft sculpture; batiked cotton, silk, ultra suede, ribbon, beads, bone; each 15 in. high Photo: Allen Bryan

E

CHERILYN MARTIN
THE NETHERLANDS

Fall of Oplontis 2

Embroidery, machine quilting; silk (batik by Els van Baarle); 20 by 20 in.

Inspired by Pompei, I am attempting to recreate the ancient, decaying architecture using stitchery and color.

F

ANNE McKENZIE NICKOLSON
UNITED STATES

Beware the Monster

Embroidery; cotton floss and lace; 21 by 24¾ in.

A

TILLEKE SCHWARZ
THE NETHERLANDS

Used Cloth

Embroidery; silk, cotton, rayon,
linen, textile paint; 29½ by 27½
in. Photo: Rob Mostert

B

LINDSAY OBERMEYER
UNITED STATES

A Darning Sampler (and detail)

Darning stitches, cross stitch;
cotton floss on linen;
11¼ by 17⅞ in. Photo: Kildow

*While the text could easily be
taken from an embroidery manual, except for the word suture, it
is taken from a 1974 surgical
manual. The most precious cloth
to stitch is human skin.*

A

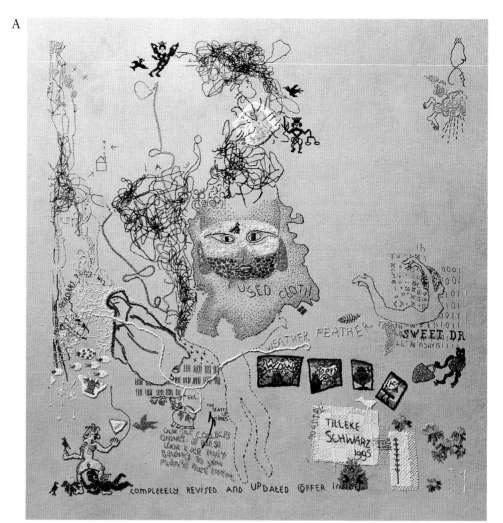

B

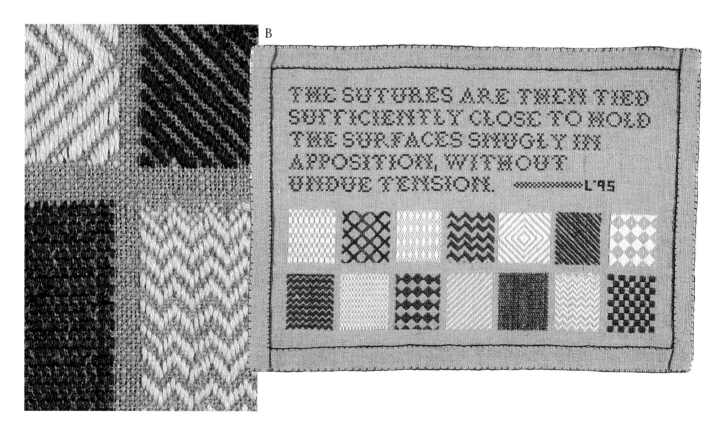

C

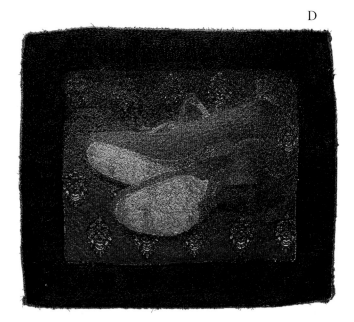

C

Meta R. Ayers
UNITED STATES

Pocahontas as the Corn Maiden

Canvas embroidery; cotton, wool, silk; 16 by 16¼ in.

Pocahontas is my ancester and I wanted to honor her spirit with this portrait.

D

Sharon Peoples
AUSTRALIA

Red Shoes on Rug

Machine embroidery; rayon, polyester, cotton; 12 by 18 in. Photo: Matt Kelso

Putting on red shoes helps one to feel good and is symbolic of taking control of one's life.

E

Ursula C. McCarty
UNITED STATES

Building Your Personality
I-IV (and detail)

Embroidery; linen; each panel 12 by 10 in. Photo: Mark Tade

As I become more involved in studying the sampler tradition, I am learning how the making of samplers and other embroidered domestic objects was used to inculcate "feminine" values such as patience, piety, filial devotion, and a certain kind of patriotism. I feel a connection to the makers because these samplers record the process by which they were turned into "nice little girls." I have appropriated the sampler format in order to subvert rather than submit to this kind of training.

A

B

C

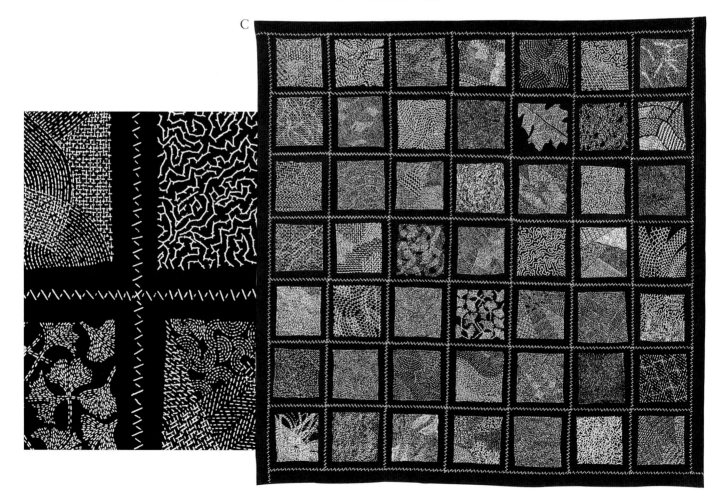

D

E

F

A

BETH BLAHUT
UNITED STATES

*Four Brains: a Threads on
the Edge Commemorative
Handkerchief*

Machine-made lace; cotton/poly-
ester sewing thread, silk;
22¼ by 20¼ in. Collection of
Helen Allen Textile Collection,
purchased with funding from the
Anonymous Fund, University of
Wisconsin–Madison.

*This work reflects my interest in
the elusive human interior, where
I find beauty and mystery. Hidden inside the body are complex
structures and systems that keep
us alive, breathing.*

B

KARIN BIRCH
UNITED STATES

Rain

Embroidery, hand stitched beadwork; linen, beads, acrylic paint;
12 by 8 by 1½ in.

C

BARBARA SCHULMAN
UNITED STATES

49 Vignettes on Turning 50
(and detail)

Hand stitching, dyeing, piecing;
pearl cotton on industrial wool
felt; 67½ by 67 in.
Photo: Robert Walc

D

ELS VAN BAARLE
THE NETHERLANDS

Hier Rust V

Embroidery, painting; cotton,
paper, plastic; 19¾ by 23¾ in.
Photo: Riny Sluys

E

BERNADETTE (B.G.)
BRADSHAW
UNITED STATES

The End of the Buffet Line

Free-motion machine embroidery;
polyester thread on muslin; 18⅜
by 29⅜ in.

*I look forward to being an age
when my only worries will be
having lunch on time and being
at the front of the buffet line.*

F

ANNIE SCHÖNLAU
GERMANY

*Entrance into the hidden
mystery*

Machine embroidery, painting;
sewing yarn; 40½ by 63½ in.

A

LINDA BEHAR
UNITED STATES

Wingaersheek Rocks III
Embroidery; fabric, thread, paint;
4 by 5 in. Photo: David Caras,
collection of Kathy Berkman

B

LINDA BEHAR
UNITED STATES

Salt Marsh V
Embroidery; fabric, thread, paint;
3⅞ by 5¾ in.
Photo: David Caras

C

CAROL SHINN
UNITED STATES

Agave
Machine embroidery; cotton; 7½
by 11 in.

*To achieve the freedom I want
with the sewing machine, I lower
the feed dog so the machine does
not control the fabric. I layer
and mix different colors of
thread throughout each piece. I
allow the distortion that occurs
in the embroidery process to be a
part of the finished work because
I like the emphasis it places on
the stitching process.*

A

B

C

D

D

B. J. Adams
UNITED STATES

A Personal Paradox
Machine embroidery; wool, net,
paper; 18 by 23½ in. Photo:
Breger and Associates

*The paradox is to be part of a
completed still life of a work,
still in progress.*

E

Carol Shinn
UNITED STATES

Early Morning
Machine embroidery; cotton;
16¾ by 18¼ in.

E

A

Beth Nobles
UNITED STATES

Route 66 Map Book (detail)
Embroidery, beadwork, silk painting, photo transfer; cotton, silk, glass beads; 4½ by 7 by 1 in. (has four 4 by 6 in. pages) Photo: Jon Van Allen

I grew up on Route 66, and it is in my soul.

B

Jan Schlieper
UNITED STATES

Night Sky of Destiny

Thread tufting; cotton and metallic floss; 4½ by 6 in. Photo: Jim Schlieper

C

Judith Tomlinson Trager
UNITED STATES

Retablo al Pescado Muerto
Machine embroidery and piecing, applique, assemblage; commercial fabrics, found objects; 24 by 30 by 4 in. Photo: Robin Taylor Daugherty

This is from the series, "Plastic Flowers in a Mexican Graveyard," which celebrates the thread of memory, the complexity of fusion, and the joy of the Mexican-American culture.

A

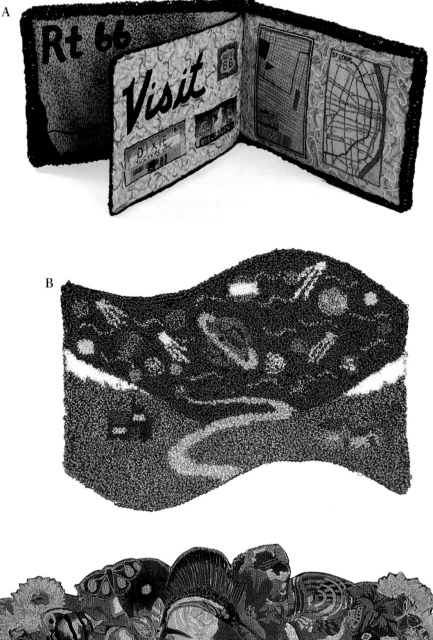

B

C

D

D

MARYELLEN SINCLAIR
UNITED STATES

Hair Net (detail)
Stitchery, wrapping; constructed box, cotton, stiffened felt, ribbon; full piece 4 by 6 by 1½ in.

My work is the result of a lifetime's fascination with thread. This simple line spun of fiber defines its own rules.

E

BETTE USCOTT-WOOLSEY
UNITED STATES

Patchwork #8
Embroidery, piecing, painting; thread, silk; 32 by 44 in. Photo: Will Brown

E

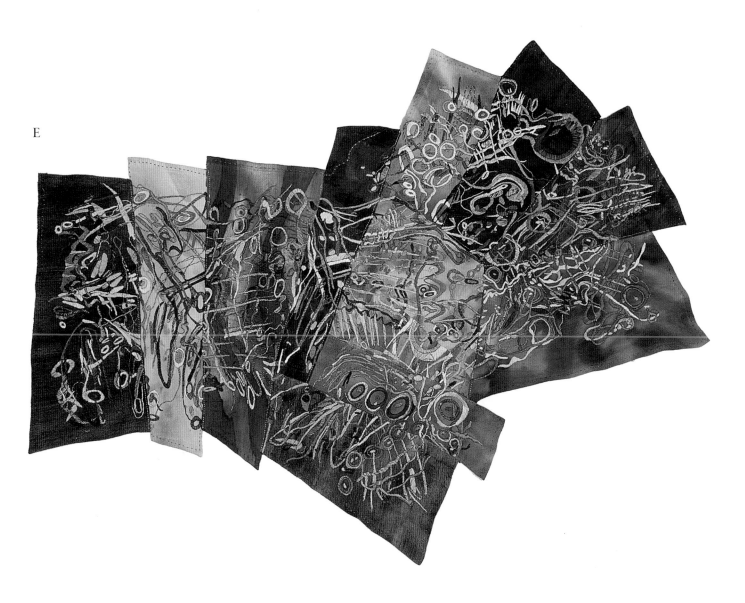

A

MARI BETH BALOGA
UNITED STATES

Grass
Hand and machine embroidery;
cotton, heat transfer print;
15 by 17 in.

B

BENTE ODNER
NORWAY

*Autumn and Spring, Hvaler,
Norway*
Applique, embroidery, knitting;
fabric, yarn; 34 by 39 in.

*The red building is the school
from the early 19th century,
when it was also the teacher's
home, the bank, and the post
office. The "new" school (background) was built in 1893.*

A

B

C

RIKI ZARRIS
UNITED STATES

Baby Boy
Embroidery; cotton; 6¼ by 4½
in. Photo: Taylor Dabney

D

ROB WATT
UNITED STATES

Winter Light
Embroidery; cotton thread on
silk; 6 by 9 in.

E

CHRISTA CORNER
ENGLAND

Malabar Spice Trader
Embroidery, hand and machine
stitching; brown wrapping paper;
8 by 13½ in.

*I did the piece after a journey
through southern India.*

A

BETTE LEVY
UNITED STATES

Crinoidial Bliss
Embroidery; silk; 15 by 20 in.
Photo: Dawghaus

*Based on prehistoric sea lilies
called crinoids, this piece refers to
the interdependence and interre-
latedness of all life forms.*

B

MARI BETH BALOGA
UNITED STATES

The Sky's the Limit
Embroidery; tapestry and hard-
ware cloth; 12 by 12 in.

A

B

C

C

MARTY JONAS
UNITED STATES

Gabbeh Carpet
Embroidery; layered commercial
fabrics; 18½ by 25 in. Photo:
Heidi Desuyo

D

PAMELA SCHLOFF
UNITED STATES

Midwest Mecca (and detail)
Construction, sewing; cotton,
beads, found objects; 24 by 24 by
2 in. Photo: Nel Ytsma

D

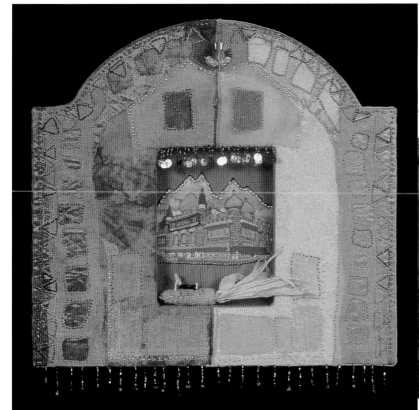

A

B

A

ELLY SMITH
UNITED STATES

Exposure (and detail)
Counted thread; cotton and
metallic thread; 40 by 52 in.

B

RACHEL COLEMAN
ENGLAND

**The Mischievous Rabbit and
Telephone 1**
Applique, hand and machine
embroidery; silk, hand-dyed fabric; 30 by 18 in.

*My rabbit always found a way to
destroy my phone, especially
while I was using it!*

QUILTS

JANE BURCH COCHRAN
UNITED STATES

Looking for God

Machine pieced, hand appliqued; commercial fabric, beads, paint, found objects;
74 by 64 in. Photo: Pam Monfort

I had fun making this quilt. I even said aloud,
"I don't care if anyone likes this quilt; I like it."

A

Susan Rienzo
UNITED STATES

Coffee House
Random pieced, hand appliqued, machine quilted; cotton; 41 by 46 in. Photo: Karen Bell

B

Sarah J. Gindel
UNITED STATES

Spirits III
Machine pieced and quilted, hand appliqued; cotton; 66 by 51 in. Photo: David Caras

This quilt evolved from a drawing of African masks at the Fogg Museum in Cambridge, Massachusetts.

C

Natasha Kempers-Cullen
UNITED STATES

Joie de Vivre
Machine pieced, appliqued, quilted, hand beaded; hand-painted and commercial fabric, glass beads, found objects; 55 by 66 in. Photo: Dennis Griggs

This quilt is dedicated to my Mom. She had an amazing, energetic love of life!

A

C

B

D

D

SALLY BROADWELL
UNITED STATES

Shoot the Moon
Hand and machine pieced, hand quilted, photo transfer; commercial fabric, beads, found objects; 39 by 35 in.

E

ANNE TRIGUBA
UNITED STATES

Markers
Machine pieced, hand appliqued and quilted; cotton; 39 by 32 in.

A whole series of quilts came about after I visited Indian graveyards in Taos, New Mexico.

E

A

A

Michael James
UNITED STATES

Hive

Machine pieced and quilted; hand-dyed and commercial cotton; 44 by 65½ in. Photo: David Caras

B

Dorle Stern-Straeter
GERMANY

In the Reed

Crazy quilt technique; cotton, silk; 60 by 55 in. Photo: Patricia Fliegauf

A visit to the reed region of northern Germany inspired this quilt.

B

C

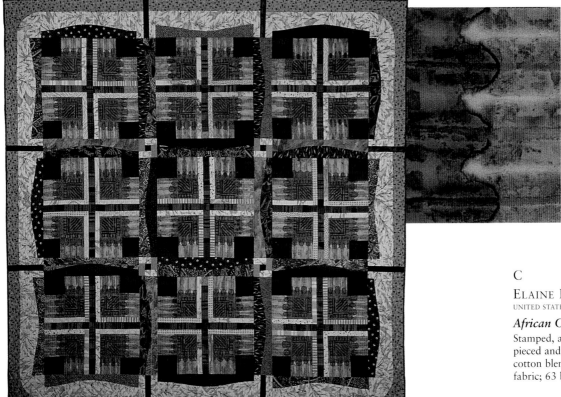

D

C

ELAINE PLOGMAN
UNITED STATES

African Crosses *(and detail)*
Stamped, air brushed, machine
pieced and quilted; cotton,
cotton blends, African tie-dyed
fabric; 63 by 63 in.

D

JILL PACE
UNITED STATES

Heaven's Gate
Machine pieced, hand appliqued,
quilted, and embroidered; cotton;
82 by 82 in.

*I was inspired to make the piece
after seeing a television program
about near-death experiences.
Everyone described themselves as
floating down a corridor with
colorful squares of light and the
glowing outline of a figure
reaching out to them.*

A

Heather W. Tewell
UNITED STATES

Old Growth and Salal
Machine pieced and quilted; cotton; 61 by 89 in. Photo: Charles Crust

Douglas firs show their age up close: long, barren trunks, branches missing and broken off, they appear to be gruff statues soaring to the clouds. Salal, also native to the state of Washington, thrives in their protection.

B

Katy Korkos
UNITED STATES

The Great Unconformity
Pieced, quilted, painted; hand-dyed cotton, sun-painted fabric; 53 by 23 in. Photo: Hawthorne Studio

The Great Unconformity is a geological formation in the Grand Canyon. I hoped to show the visual representation of time in this quilt.

B

A

C

D

E

F

C
BONNIE JEAN THORNTON
UNITED STATES

Sylvan Ballet

Machine pieced and quilted;
cyanotype prints, hand-dyed and
commercial fabric; 42 by 29 in.
Photo: J. W. Thornton

*As I walk through the woods and
see magnificent sword ferns
moving in a slight breeze, I think
of graceful ballet dancers. I tried
to capture that rhythm in this
piece.*

D
AMY GRABEL
UNITED STATES

Franklin Park

Machine pieced and quilted,
painted; cotton; 20 by 28 in.
Photo: David Caras

E
MARY GATTIS
UNITED STATES

Forecast

Machine pieced and quilted,
photo silkscreen, painted; cotton,
drapery fabric, taffeta, paper; 32
by 48 in. Photo: David Caras

F
ELAINE CAMPBELL
AUSTRALIA

Hamersley Ranges Revisited

Machine pieced, hand quilted,
machine and hand embroidered;
painted and dyed fabric, wool;
24 by 24 in. Photo: Doug
Campbell

A

LINDA CHRISTMAN
UNITED STATES

Take Time

Hand and machine quilted, photo transfer, machine appliqued, painted; hand-dyed cotton and vintage fabric; 40 by 58 in.

The imagery signifies just a few of life's pleasures that we take for granted. This quilt is meant to be a pleasant reminder for all of us to stop for a moment and "take time to smell the roses."

B

KARLA DE KETELAERE
SPAIN

Tears of the Desert

Quilted, batiked; silk; 19 by 36 in.

C

PAT HEWITT
NEW ZEALAND

Alien Star Signs

Machine pieced, quilted, and embroidered, painted; cotton and synthetic fabric; 44 by 32 in.
Photo: Gilbert van Reenen

I am convinced there are life forms out there in space. Maybe they have a calendar with birth signs similar to these.

A

B

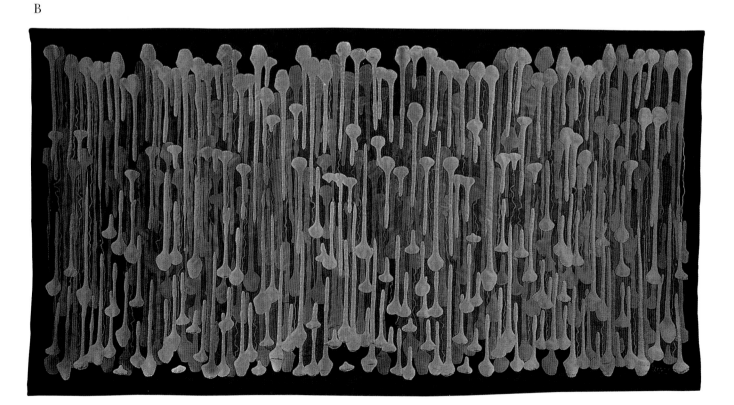

C

D

E

D

HAZEL AYRE HYNDS
UNITED STATES

The Mind Is A Terrible Thing To Waste II
Machine appliqued and quilted, hand embellished; hand-dyed and commercial cotton, paper, brass; 37 by 26 in.

This deals with the fragmentation so many people experience in today's society. While the clock ticks away the hours, days, and years, we desperately seek wholeness of body, mind, and spirit.

E

SALLY SCOTT
SOUTH AFRICA

Nightfall Over Malilangwe
(and detail)
Machine appliqued, hand quilted; hand-dyed cotton and commercial fabric; 42 by 18 in.

A

Rachel S. Kitterman
UNITED STATES

Forest House

Machine pieced and quilted,
reverse hand appliqued;
discharge-dyed cotton; 28½ by
34½ in. Photo: Curtis Almquist

*The design came from the desire
to get back to a more simple,
elemental quilting style. For me,
the most important architecture
is a simple house that is in tune
with nature. To that end, I
wanted my quilt house to be not
only in the forest but of the
forest.*

B

Barbara Lydecker Crane
UNITED STATES

Ombu Tree

Hand pieced, appliqued, and
quilted; hand-dyed and
commercial cotton; 69 by 55½ in.
Photo: David Caras

A

B

C

C

LAURA WASILOWSKI
UNITED STATES

Gardening Tip #3: Tools
Fused applique, machine quilted;
hand-dyed and commercial
cotton; 53 by 45 in. Photo:
Melody Johnson

D

JANE A. SASSAMAN
UNITED STATES

Brambles
Machine appliqued and quilted;
cotton; 24 by 24 in. Photo:
Gregory Gantner

E

REE NANCARROW
UNITED STATES

Fall Tundra
Machine pieced and quilted
(quilted by Wynona Harris King);
cotton; 71 by 72 in.

D

E

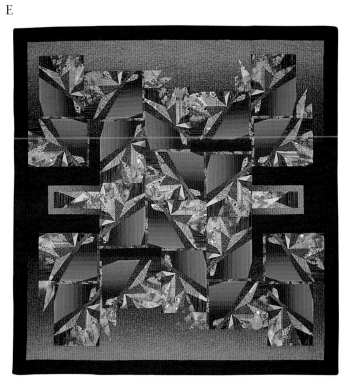

A

Janet Kurjan
UNITED STATES

Carreau IV
Machine pieced and quilted; hand-dyed and commercial cotton; 51 by 49 in. Photo: Jeff Clarke

My background in genetics, a science of irregular patterns, helps me work improvisationally, letting the fabric and color lead me throught a piece.

B

Robbi Joy Eklow
UNITED STATES

Vessels VI: Borrowed Time
Fused applique, machine quilted; hand-dyed cotton; 55 by 67 in.

The clock was my grandmother's and it sits atop her piano in my living room. I still feel the clock and piano are hers, and I often feel that I make quilts on time borrowed from pursuits that would be more practical.

C

D

E

C

PATTY HAWKINS

UNITED STATES

Basically Scribbles
Random pieced, fused applique,
machine quilted; hand-dyed and
painted fabric; 60 by 48 in.
Photo: Ken Sanville/Amaranth
Studios

D

SUSAN WEBB LEE

UNITED STATES

Missy's New Clothes
Quilted, embroidered, machine
pieced; hand-dyed, -painted, and
commercial cotton; 45 by 37 in.

E

CHARLOTTE YDE

DENMARK

Feeling Blue
Machine pieced and quilted,
hand appliqued; hand-dyed and
commercial cotton; 45 by 45 in.
Photo: Ulster Folk & Transport
Museum

A

KIM H. RITTER
UNITED STATES

Resurfacing
Quilted, dyed, painted; silk; 48
by 60 in. Photo: Karen Bell

B

ROBIN COWLEY
UNITED STATES

*Out of an Orange Colored
Sky*
Machine pieced, appliqued,
quilted; hand-dyed and
commercial cotton; 45 by 49½
in. Photo: Don Tuttle
Photography

*Sand and sea, a vacation on an
island in the middle of nowhere;
that's the dream the picture in
the calendar was selling. That
image was with me months later
as I dyed fabrics watery colors.*

A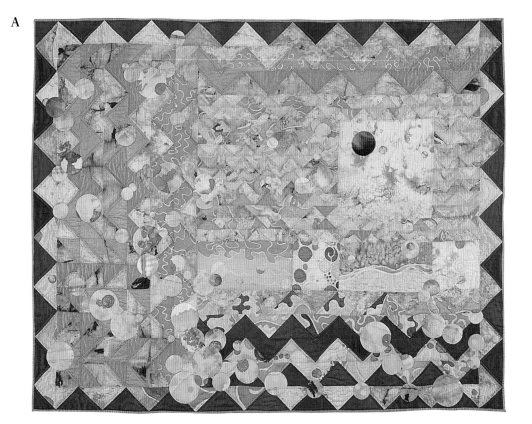

B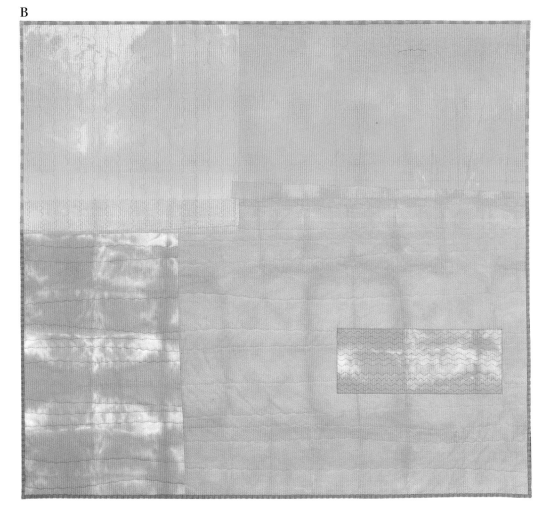

C

LINDA S. PERRY
UNITED STATES

Tales
Machine pieced and quilted, hand
appliqued, dyed, and painted;
cotton, silk, wool, linen; 78 by 59
in. Photo: Joe Ofria

D

KATHLEEN SHARP
UNITED STATES

Water Temple
Hand and machine appliqued,
pieced, embroidered, and quilted;
cotton, cotton/rayon, silk; 48 by
48 in. Photo: Richard Johns

E

LOUISE THOMPSON
UNITED STATES

Pleasure Ladies
Appliqued, hand quilted, color
Xerox transfer, marbling; cotton,
fabric paint; 60 by 80 in. Photo:
Ferrari Color

C

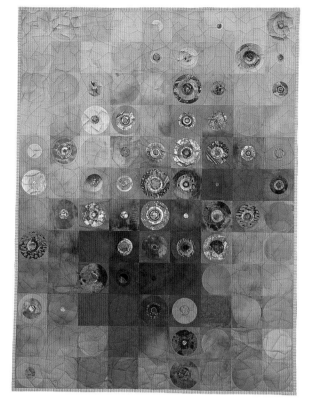

D

E

A

NELDA WARKENTIN
UNITED STATES

Yes, It's A Painting
Machine pieced and quilted,
airbrushed; cotton, acrylic paint;
60 by 60 in. Photo: John Tuckey

*I designed this quilt after
studying the work of French
artist Sonia Delaunay.*

B

MICHELE HARDY
UNITED STATES

Confetti
Machine pieced, appliqued,
quilted; hand-dyed and
commercial cotton; 44 by
51 in.

A

B

C

D

E

C

ELEANOR MCCAIN
UNITED STATES

Linear/Texture 2
Machine pieced and quilted,
painted; hand-dyed and
commercial cotton, textile paint;
36 by 28 in. Photo: Luke Jordan

D

SALLY A. SELLERS
UNITED STATES

Chamber Music
Machine appliqued onto canvas;
dyed, painted, commercial
cotton; 39½ by 35½ in.
Photo: Bill Bachhuber

E

JUTTA FARRINGER
SOUTH AFRICA

Fijnbos Garden
Machine pieced and quilted;
cotton; 33 by 35 in.
Photo: The Photographer

A

ALICE M. BEASLEY
UNITED STATES

III Boyz

Machine appliqued and quilted; cotton; 60 by 69 in. Photo: Jim Jacobs

My goal is to incorporate the same light, shadow, and perspective as artists in other media, but with the ordinary tools of a quilter, fabric and thread. All pieces are cut freehand with scissors or a rotary cutter.

B

CYNTHIA F. MYERBERG
UNITED STATES

Hidden Agenda

Machine pieced and quilted, Xerox transfer; discharge-dyed cotton, silk; 54 by 40 in. Photo: Carina Woolrich Photography

The piece explores the veiled issues present in relationships. Layering of Xerox transfer onto silk organza, cotton, and layered silk organza creates an illusive portrait.

C

JUDY ZOELZER LEVINE
UNITED STATES

Hazard

Machine pieced and quilted, stamped, painted; wool, textile ink; 29½ by 29 in.

D

for in my pocket I found the smallest piece of gold, I held it in my heart and smiled.....

D

JANINE BOYD
AUSTRALIA

Quilt for Helen
Machine embroidered and
quilted; cotton, dyed rayon
thread; 18½ by 25 in. Photo:
Grant Hancock

*This is a tribute to my mother.
The center figure is her as a
child, chosen to reflect her
vibrancy and love for life.*

E

IRENE MACWILLIAM
IRELAND

Life Goes On *(and detail)*
Machine pieced and quilted;
cotton; 64 by 64 in.

E

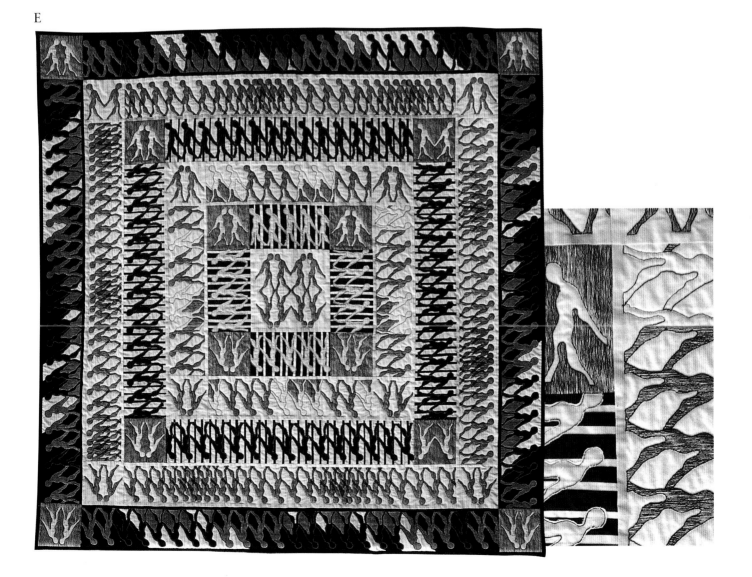

A

KAREN N. SOMA
UNITED STATES

Emergence
Machine quilted and
embroidered, beaded; screen
printed and hand-dyed cotton,
found objects; 18 by 18 in.
Photo: Mark Frey

*I started thinking about the many
roles that stand between women
and their creative core—those
patterns of behavior we welcome
and those we resist. Here the core
is covered by another, barely
transparent pattern, now
protected from those who would
"X" out its potential, emerging
from behind yet another mask to
join an ongoing current of
possibilities.*

B

PAULA NADELSTERN
UNITED STATES

*Kaleidoscopic XVIII:
Caribbean Blues*
Machine pieced and quilted;
cotton, silk; 71 by 66 in. Photo:
Karen Bell

*Eight months after a book
deadline, a broken ankle, college
applications, and a record-
breaking New York City winter,
we fell side by side on the beach
in Cancun and watched our blues
turn into other blues.*

A

B

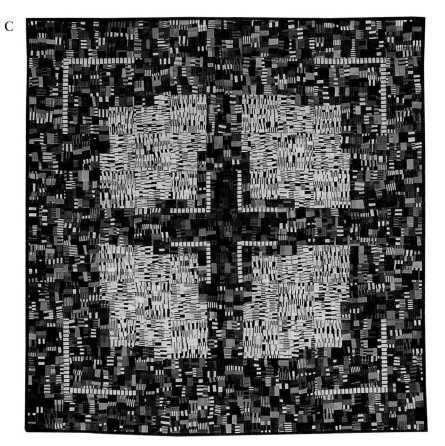

C

C
Ruth Garrison
UNITED STATES

Staccato 4
Machine pieced and quilted, screen printed; cotton; 48 by 48 in.

D
Ann Harwell
UNITED STATES

Hurricane Fran/Chaotic Symmetry
Machine pieced, hand quilted; cotton; 54 by 54 in. Photo: Lynn Ruck

My mission is to create order from chaos, to unite and enhance diverse fabric designs and colors with intricate quilting.

D

A

Carolyn L. Mazloomi
UNITED STATES

Daughter of the Sun

Appliqued, reverse appliqued;
silk, batik, African cotton, beads,
shells; 72 by 72 in. Photo:
Charles E. Martin

*This quilt is from a series of 16
made to commemorate the
United Nations Conference for
Women that was held in Beijing.*

B

**Sandra Townsend
Donabed**

UNITED STATES

*Jitterbug Waltz, Fats Waller,
1942*

Hand and reverse appliqued and
quilted; African cotton, other
commercial fabric; 43 by 43 in.
Photo: David Caras

A

B

C

D

E

C

BARBARA BUTLER
UNITED STATES

Uncertain Journey

Machine pieced, appliqued,
quilted; cotton; 42½ by 28½ in.
Photo: Jeff Kanupp

D

SANDI CUMMINGS AND SANDY KLOP
UNITED STATES

Woman in Repose

Machine pieced, appliqued,
quilted; hand-dyed and
commercial cotton; 76 by 53 in.
Photo: Don Tuttle

E

LISSA VALENTINE
UNITED STATES

Madonna

Machine pieced, appliqued,
quilted; cotton, gold trim; 66 by
90 in. Photo: Ross Mulhausen

A

B

C

A

LINDA ROBINSON
UNITED STATES

Seldovia
Hand and machine pieced and
quilted, painted; hand-dyed and
commercial cotton, handmade
paper, acrylic paint; 42 by 36 in.
Photo: Craig Freas

*Alaska has a wealth of
waterfront communities, and
Seldovia is among my favorites.
Only accessible by water or air, it
is located on Kachemak Bay and
is home to about "307 friendly
people and a few old crabs."*

B

SCHNUPPE VON GWINNER
GERMANY

Night Lights
Patchwork; painted and
commercial fabric; 47¼ by 55¼ in.

*This is my homage to nights in
Hamburg.*

C

CAROL ANNE GROTRIAN
UNITED STATES

*Crystalline Morning,
Midsummer's Night*
Hand and machine pieced and
quilted, shibori, hand stamped;
cotton, fiber reactive dyes, fabric
paint; each panel 24 by 72 in.
Photo: David Caras

D

E

F

D

JUDI H. BASTION
UNITED STATES

Metropolis
Hand and machine pieced, hand quilted; cotton, beads; 38 by 37 in. Photo: LeeAnn Lafleur

A cartoon by Ever Muelen in The New Yorker *challenged me to do this quilt.*

E

LAUREN CAMP
UNITED STATES

That Light Sort of Rain
Machine pieced and quilted; cotton, silk, rayon, velvet; 70½ by 63 in. Photo: Hawthorne Studio

New York is fast, angry, unknowable; it is also bright, exciting, and powerful. Late to a show, hungry, and hoping to hail a cab one blustery, drizzly, gray day, I watched in frustration as each "off duty" taxi passed me by.

F

DOMINIE NASH
UNITED STATES

Red Landscape I
Machine appliqued, machine and hand quilted, screen printed, monoprinted; fiber reactive dyes, cotton, silk, textile paint; 41 by 61 in.

A

GENEVIEVE ATTINGER
FRANCE

Aux creux des caves

Machine pieced, appliqued, and
embroidered, hand quilted;
commercial fabric; 51 by 55 in.
Photo: Jacques Marie Dit-Dinard

*My grandparents made wine,
and the wine cellar was a warm,
convivial place where friends
came to taste the fruits of the
harvest.*

B

ELLEN ADAMS
CANADA

Don't Play With Your Food

Appliqued, quilted; commercial
fabric; 33½ by 58 in.

*A game is in progress on a
chessboard, with the chess pieces
represented by items of food. An
earthquake has ripped through
the board, making the pawns
(prawns) nervous, which they
express by beating each other up
and pushing other pieces over the
brink, where they turn into
trout-like fish.*

C

C

WENDY JORDAN
UNITED STATES

Lean Into It
Machine pieced and quilted;
hand-dyed and commercial
cotton; 29¼ by 52 in. Photo:
Christopher Jordan

*Have you ever been
simultaneously afraid of change,
yet afraid nothing would change?
Do you experience moments
when your feelings frighten you?
Are you so amazed and awed by
the wonder of life that you fear
time might run out before you get
it all?*

D

KATIE PASQUINI
MASOPUST
UNITED STATES

Grapes
Machine appliqued and quilted;
cotton blends; 96 by 70 in.
Photo: Hawthorne Studio,
collection of The Hendrex'

D

A

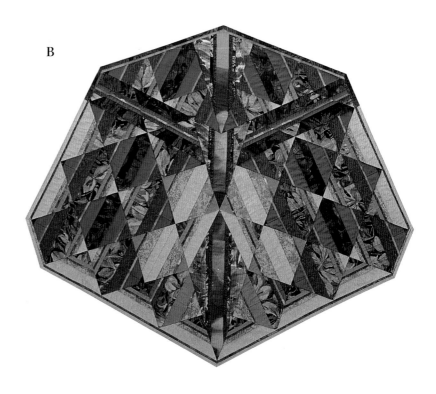

B

C

A

JUDY BECKER
UNITED STATES

Uneasy Balance
Pieced, quilted; cotton; 64 by 48
in. Photo: David Caras

B

JANE HYER WALTON
UNITED STATES

Lady of the Lake
Machine pieced and quilted;
cotton; 40 by 46½ in. Photo: Jim
Buivid

C

ANNE-MARIE STEWART

ENGLAND

Reverberations – Roses
Machine pieced, appliqued, and
quilted; hand-dyed and
commercial cotton, ribbon
snippets; 52 by 52 in. Photo:
Richard Stewart

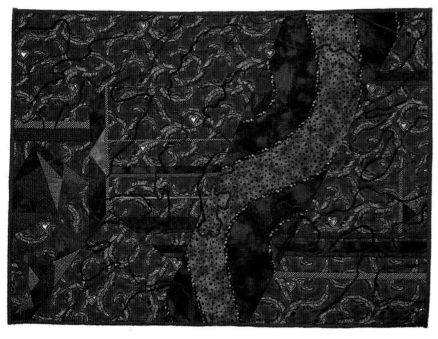

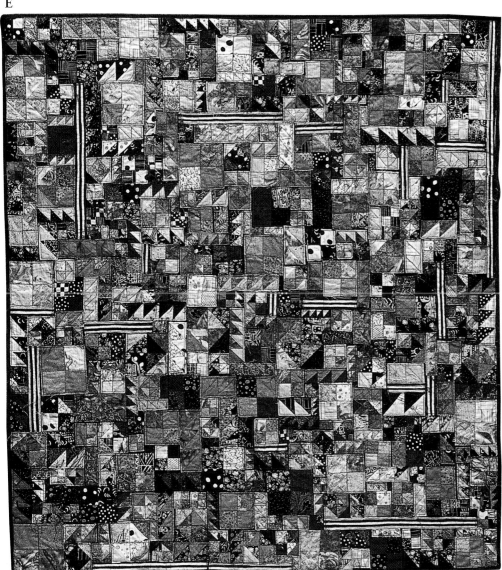

D

SHIRLEY CONNOLLY
CANADA

Frog Room
Machine pieced and appliqued, hand sewn hearts; cotton, wool, bronze; 37¼ by 34¾ in. Photo: Sundog Photo

E

TOOT REID
UNITED STATES

Seven
Machine pieced and appliqued, hand quilted; cotton; 62 by 57½ in. Photo: Ken Wagner

A

SUSAN SHIE AND
JAMES ACORD
UNITED STATES

Daddy's Little Pumpkin

Machine sewn and quilted, hand-
and airbrush-painted; commercial
fabric, fabric paint; 44½ by 42½
in. Collection of Elizabeth Cherry
Owen, Baton Rouge, Louisiana

B

SHARON KING
UNITED STATES

Jumanji

Machine quilted, hand beadwork
and batik; 23½ by 60½ in. Photo:
Charley Freiberg

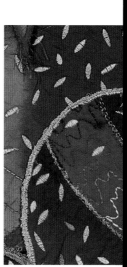

C

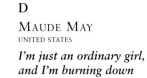

C

SHARON M. COMMINS
UNITED STATES

Exuberance (and detail) ©1997
Machine appliqued, embroidered,
and quilted; cotton; 50 by 30 in.

*This is for my free-spirited
daughter, who leads with her
heart.*

D

D

MAUDE MAY
UNITED STATES

***I'm just an ordinary girl,
and I'm burning down
the house*** (and detail)
Machine and hand quilted and
appliqued, airbrushed, color
transfer; hand-dyed and
commercial fabric; 24 by 36 in.
Photo: Mark Frey, collection of
Warren and Nancy Brakenseik,
Los Angeles

*I was playing Bonnie Raitt's
version of David Byrne's song
and this quilt resulted. The
women and girls are members of
my family and extended family.*

E

GERRY CHASE
UNITED STATES

Sampler IV: Play TV
Machine pieced and quilted,
painted; commercial fabric, ink,
pastel, acrylic paint; 46 by 59 in.
Photo: Roger Schreiber

*We can display our inner selves
on the public stage as though it
were, well, as easy as being in a
soap opera.*

A

B

A

MARY CATHERINE LAMB
UNITED STATES

Apocalyptic Dragon
Machine pieced, appliqued,
embroidered, and quilted; vintage
drapery fabric, Japanese silk,
African tie-dyed brocade, cotton,
metallics; 36 by 28 in.
Photo: Bill Bachhuber

B

SANDRA HOEFNER
UNITED STATES

Catnap
Hand appliqued and quilted;
cotton, piping; 65 by 45 in.
Photo: Brian Allen

*My cat, Capezio, is dreaming of
the animals he dispatched during
a long and successful hunting
career. I did this portrait after he
died.*

C

CARYL GAUBATZ
UNITED STATES

Giraffe
Machine pieced and quilted, hand
appliqued, painted; commercial
batik, fabric paint; 31¼ by 32 in.
Photo: Gary Gaubatz

C

CATHERINE K
AUSTRALIA
Precious News
Pleating; newsprint, box; box, 4 by 4 in., newsprint, 3¾ by 119 in.
Photo: Tim Brook

A

A

KATHLEEN HOLMES
UNITED STATES

Acme Angel
Construction; paper, found textiles, sheet metal, paint; 32 by 18 by 10 in.

B

JANE DUNNEWOLD AND BARBARA LEE SMITH
UNITED STATES

Red Ladder
Construction, machine stitched; interfacing; 11 by 14 by 2 in. Photo: Michael Smith

C

MARY ZENA
UNITED STATES

Mycomium Rouge
Machine stitched; commercial fabric; 5 by 4½ by 2¾ in. Photo: Geoffrey Carr

D

HELENA HYYRYLAINEN
FINLAND

Coral
Burning; polyester fabric; 102 by 39½ in. diameter

E

DIXIE D. BROWN
UNITED STATES

Chrysalis (and detail)
Plaiting, layering; reed, gut; 12 by 20 by 8 in. Photo: Gugger Petter

When my last child left the nest, I created this emptied but exuberant form.

F

TERESA PLA BELIO
SPAIN

Espiral
Plaiting; cotton; full installation, 48 in. diameter

I did 27 cubes for this installation. Color and delicate textures are very important to me, and I am very interested in non-loom textile techniques.

B

C

D

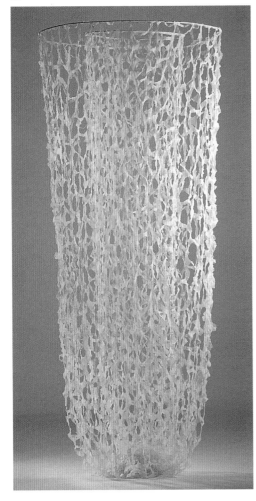

E

F

A

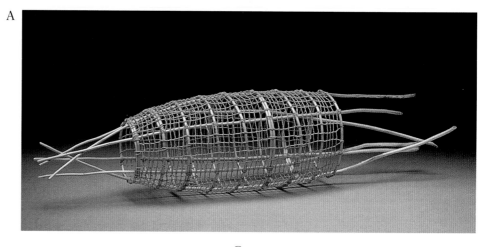

A

KRISTA SPIELER
UNITED STATES

Spirit's Release
Lashed construction, weft
wrapping; willow, waxed linen;
7 by 8 by 20 in. Photo: Peter Lee

*I learned about the weft wrapping
technique in Ed Rossbach's book,*
Baskets as Textile Art. *This image
came to me around the time of
my father's death, and is in
memory of his passage.*

B

VIRGINIA KAISER
AUSTRALIA

Light Over Dark
Woven, painted; paper, paper
bark, cane, acrylic paint; 12 by 5
in. diameter Photo: Greg Piper

C

JAN HOPKINS
UNITED STATES

Transformation Vessel
Stitched, looped, molded, formed;
agave leaves, lotus pod tops,
waxed linen, sweet grass, cedar
root, magnolia leaves, paper, bull
kelp; 9 by 10 by 11 in. Photo:
Jerry McCollum, collection of
Mr. and Mrs. Eric Barkan

D

FRAN REED
UNITED STATES

Halibut Seed II, I, IV, III
Stitched; halibut skin, gut,
willow, leaves; 12 by 10 by 11 in.
to 14 by 24 by 23 in.
Photo: Chris Arend

B

C

D

E

E

SUE KOLVEREID
UNITED STATES

Lake Bed Series I
Weaving, twining; cedar bark, freshwater rush, found wood; 12 by 10½ by 7½ in. Photo: Bruce Blank

F

POLLY JACOBS
GIACCHINA
UNITED STATES

Civilization
Twining; date palm seed frond, willow, waxed linen; 41 by 14 by 7 in. Photo: Rodney Nakamoto Photography

G

REGULA ALLENSPACH
WEILL
UNITED STATES

Dogwood Barking at Red "Moons" in Elliptical Orbits
Construction; dogwood branches, cedar shavings, grapevine balls, wire; 45 by 28 by 28 in. Photo: Gugger Petter

Structure, movement, balance, and nature's gifts are combined in this free-standing sculpture. I felt, since we multiply so many other "things" in life, that I could clone my red moons and let them flow through the elements.

F

G

A

ROB DOBSON
UNITED STATES

Basket #23
Hand and machine stitched,
twining; recycled envelopes,
electric wire; 9 by 15 by 15 in.
Photo: Steve Gyurina

B

LINDA FIFIELD
UNITED STATES

Earth and Fire IX
Netting stitch over lathe-turned
vessel; Czech glass seed beads,
wood; 11 by 8 by 8 in. Photo:
Jack Fifield

C

JO STEALEY
UNITED STATES

Urbanscape
Stitched, stenciled, collaged;
handmade paper, acrylic paint;
36 by 10 by 10 in.
Photo: Jim Curley

A

B

C

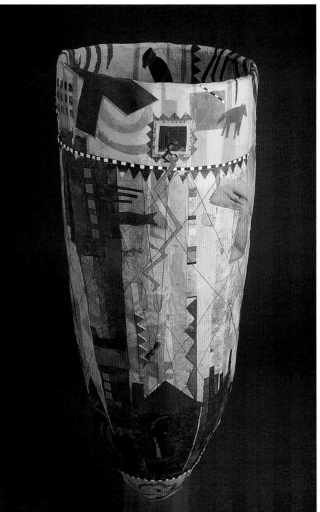

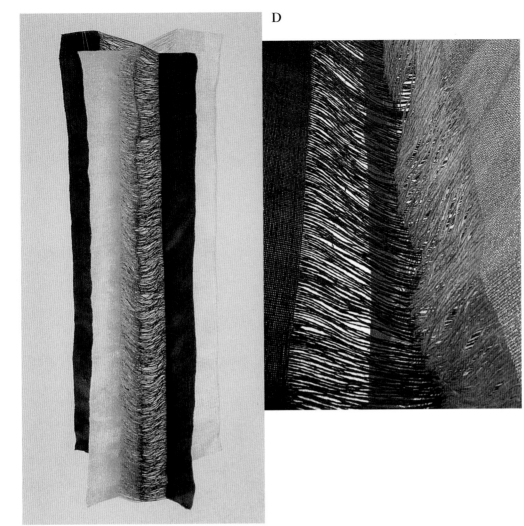

D

D

EWHA KWEON
GERMANY

Light and Shadow III (and detail)

Double plain weave; wool, linen;
37 by 20 by 20 in.

*I use a double weave technique,
weaving two layers
simultaneously, one upon the
other. I guide the underlayer
through the overlayer and thereby
effect a change in the surface.*

E

MAUREEN E. KELLY
UNITED STATES

Rockefeller

Appliqued design stretched onto
frame; sunbrella fabric;
11 by 14 ft. Photo: Sue Sonz

E

A

A

NANCY JONES WETMORE
UNITED STATES

, Inc.

Handwoven, stitched; copper and
steel wire; 60 by 36 in. diameter
Photo: Matt McFarland

*We perceive ourselves as free
from oppressive attitudes yet we
willingly don the mythic
garments that propagate the
stereotype. What is "femininity"
but the propagation of a myth?*

B

CATHRYN MALLORY
UNITED STATES

Fissure

Crochet, stitching, wrapping;
screen mesh, wire, copper tubing;
29 by 15 by 16 in.
Photo: Carl Basner

*I work in an intuitive manner,
utilizing traditional fiber
techniques to transform recycled
and found materials into vessel
forms with visually active
surfaces.*

B

C

JACQUELINE DOYLE-
DREWES
UNITED STATES

***And I bring them gifts of
my soul...***

Wrapped, woven, stitched,
painted; plastic mesh, metallic
ribbon, lint, glass, acrylic paint;
57 by 17 by 10 in.
Photo: Bob Elbert

*One recurring theme in my work
that synthesizes the idea of
confinement is the Egyptian
mummy form. I hope to elicit an
eerie, other-worldly feeling, and
an element of mystery through
the effects of light and shadow.*

C

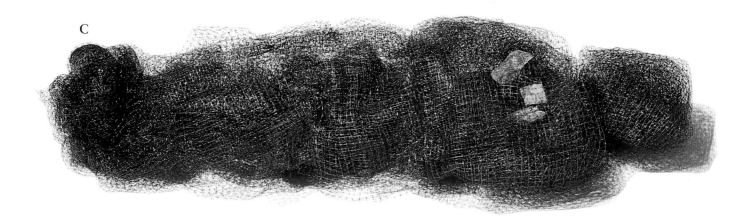

D

D

DONALD TALBOT
UNITED STATES

Family Ties

Construction; bronze mesh, copper
foil, wire; 36 by 25 by 4 in.

*The piece is about our patriarchal
society and men standing
"shoulder-to-shoulder" as a
means of self-preservation, self-
assertion, and male bonding.*

E

JACKIE ABRAMS
UNITED STATES

Copper Moonlight

Painted, stitched; paper, waxed
linen, copper, varnish; 16 by 10
by 10 in. Photo: Greg Hubbard

F

FLO BARRY
UNITED STATES

Treasure Book from the Digs

Weaving; dyed fabric, wire, beads,
metal; 15 by 20 in. diameter

*After seeing the findings from
archaeological digs, I was inspired
to create my interpretation.*

E

F

A

JOHN L. SKAU
UNITED STATES

Red and Blue Vortex

Damask weave; maple, poplar, wood dye; 19 by 24 by 24 in.

B

ELAINE SMALL
UNITED STATES

Phantom Voyage

Knotting; waxed linen, mirror base; 13½ by 5¾ by 3½ in.
Photo: Red Elf, Inc.

C

BILLIE RUTH SUDDUTH
UNITED STATES

The Golden Ratio

Hand-dyed twill weave construction; reed, walnut hull and iron oxide dye; 18 by 17 by 17 in. Photo: Robert Chiarito

D

FLO HOPPE
UNITED STATES

Intermezzo

3-rod wale, randing, embroidery; rattan, cane; 14 by 8 in. diameter
Photo: John C. Keys

E

NANCY MOORE BESS
UNITED STATES

Jar from Kawagoe to New York

Twining, plaiting; waxed cotton and linen, vintage netsuke; 3½ by 5 in. diameter
Photo: D. James Dee

F

ZOE MORROW
UNITED STATES

Cashing In

Weaving; shredded money; 10 by 7½ x 9¼ in. Photo: Charles H. Jenkins

G

LIZ STOEHR
UNITED STATES

Black Braided Form #7

Plainweave, stitching; braided elastic; 6 by 2½ in. diameter

A

B

C

D

E

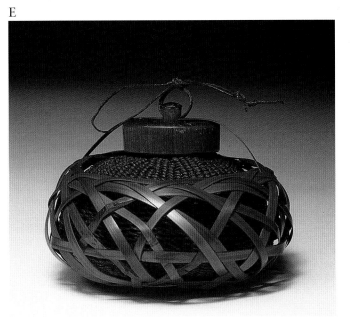

F

G

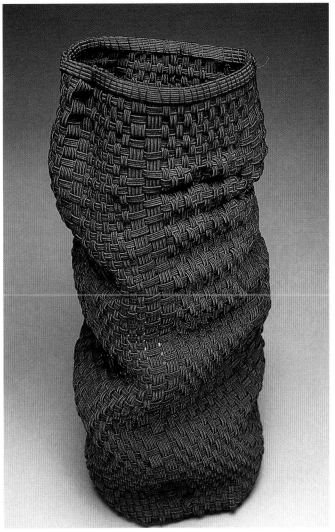

A

JUDY BALES
UNITED STATES

Property Lines II
Wrapping, painting, stitching;
fabric, wire fencing, aluminum
screen, plastic coated wire; 22 by
20 by 9 in. Photo: Michael
Kreiser

*I am intrigued by the use of cold,
industrial materials to create
objects that contain warmth and
lyricism.*

B

JUDY L. KAHLE
UNITED STATES

The World Needs More...
Machine stitched, photo transfer,
collage; satin, canvas; 12 by 6 by
8 in. Photo: Jerry L. Anthony

*This piece came about after I
stopped neighborhood children
from chasing the wild animals I
feed in my backyard. I decided
that the world needed more acts
of kindness and that I would
create a vessel to hold them.*

C

NanC MEINHARDT
UNITED STATES

Let Me Out
Off-loom weaving; glass and gold
seed beads, silk, wood; 10 by 5½
by 3 in. Photo: Tom Van Eynde

*The mask series addresses the
psychological inaction of a
mythical family.*

A

B

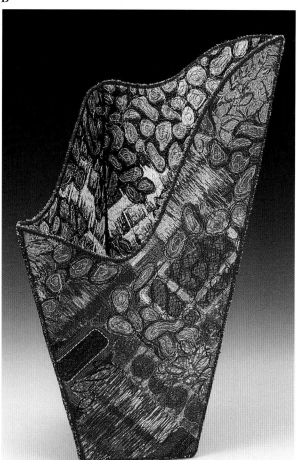

C

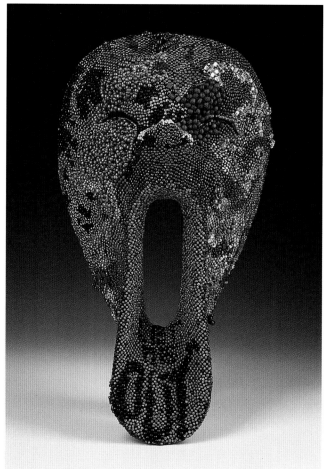

D

E

F

D

SUSAN ETCOFF
FRAERMAN
UNITED STATES

Bound for Glory
Off-loom weaving; glass seed and
metal beads, found object; 9 by
6½ by 3 in. Photo: Tom Van
Eynde

*As a child I was enthralled by
Dorothy's ruby slippers in* The
Wizard of Oz. *As a teenager, I
spent several months bound in
long leg plasters, yet conjuring
up images of myself in perilously
high heels.*

E

SALLY KNIGHT
UNITED STATES

Journey's End
Painted, stamped, collaged;
hand-painted and commercial
fabric, maps; 4¾ by 2½ by 9¾ in.
Photo: Jeff Clarke

F

KAY KHAN
UNITED STATES

Two-Handled Lidded Vessel
Construction, embroidery,
quilting, applique; felt, cotton;
7 by 16 by 14 in.
Photo: Herbert Lotz

A

ROSE KELLY
UNITED STATES

Burmese Undershirt

Weaving, stitching, collage; dress patterns, Chinese gambling forms; 22 by 32 by 1 in.

As I wove with old dress patterns, what resembled an ancient alphabet appeared. The surface reminded me of Burmese undershirts that are inscribed with protective verses.

B

LINDA LAINO
UNITED STATES

Higher Ground

Felting, plaiting, stitching; wool; 10 by 12½ by 3 in. Photo: Taylor Dabney

C

NANCY NODELMAN
UNITED STATES

There

Plaiting; painted stair treads; 8 by 8 by 1 in. Photo: Gugger Petter

D

INGE STAHL
GERMANY

Heart Constriction

Sewn, embroidered; corset, cotton; 47 by 23 by 18 in. Photo: Bruno Stahl

This is part of my "Dress Chamber" series. My work is mostly concerned with body and soul, beauty and pain.

E

CAROL DURHAM
UNITED STATES

Sticks and...

Wrapping, painting; gut, packing material, acrylic paint; 10½ by 7 by 4 in. Photo: Gugger Petter

F

LAURIE DILL-KOCHER
UNITED STATES

Portal

Random weave; abaca, hemp, pigments; 15 by 11 by 8 in.

Manipulation of materials is only the beginning of the playful approach that I have towards my work. I strive to imbue each piece with the emotional composition of nature, and to keep developing, renewing, and growing.

G

MARGARET F. CROWTHER
ENGLAND

Metamorphosis

Construction; paper yarns; 32 by 24 by 24 in.

The structural elements of the pieces are influenced by forms, rhythms, and textures of natural origin. I use mainly paper yarns and sisal, and experiment with techniques to create three-dimensional forms.

A

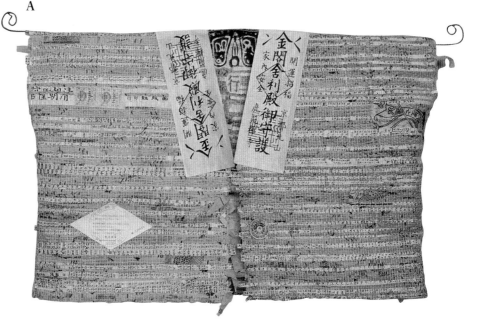

B

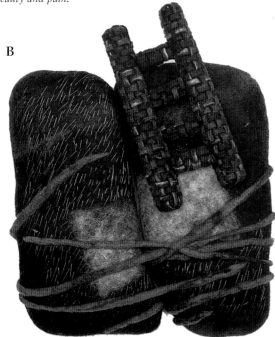

C

D

E

F

G

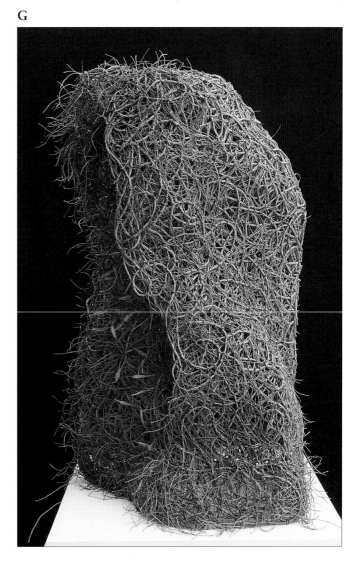

A

CHARLOTTE HAMLIN
UNITED STATES

Prayer Rug

Ghiordes knotting, dyeing, cutting; linen, cotton, wood; 56 by 76 by 22 in. Photo: Denny Moer

I have sought to depict the essence of loss. This vein of human experience never courses very far from our daily topography, and it is my nature that in order to understand and accept loss, I must dissect it. Customary activities have a new, unsolicited flavor against which we bump and struggle. We remember the last time—the conversation, the morning light, the coffee's bitterness.

B

BARBARA J. ALLEN
UNITED STATES

Spirit Dwelling: Closing the Doors

Papermaking, weaving, drawing; handmade paper, linen, ashes, gesso, graphite; 21 by 6 by 6 in. Photo: Robert Mitchell

C

AMY C. CLARKE
UNITED STATES

Sock for My Fears, Sock for My Serenity

Spinning, knitting, paper mache; wool, paper, wood; 40 by 16 by 16 in. Photo: Colorado State University Photographic Services

I use the familiar, almost mundane shape of a sock to allude to a conflict between contentment and constraint that I see in myself—wanting to love and be loved, needing independence but desiring closeness, feeling simultaneously strong and vulnerable, being both a child and an adult.

A

B

C

CARTER SMITH
UNITED STATES

Shibori Meditation Tent
Discharge dyed; silk; 10 by 10 by
11 ft. Photo: Carolyn Ross

E

GIDSKEN ELISABETH
BRAADLIE
NORWAY

Totally Coconut
Mixed techniques; coconut fiber;
large piece at far end is 6½ ft.
diameter

*The overall picture shows my
exhibition at the RAM Gallery,
Oslo, Norway. The room
dimensions are 1216 square feet.
All the works are made out of
coconut fiber, from the floor on up.*

E

A

WILLY SCHOLTEN
UNITED STATES

Leisa, President Elf Systems
Hand sewn, spray painted; metal screen, floppy disks, fabric, enamel paint; 21 by 18 by 12 in. Photo: Pat Kirk

As a Web specialist, my neighbor Leisa goes through a lot of floppy disks and attends many conferences. That's the reason for the straps from ID tags.

B

LISA LICHTENFELS
UNITED STATES

The New Guinean Warrior
Soft sculpture; nylon stockings, batting, fiberfill, wire; 16¼ by 11 by 10 in.

Fabric is not usually seen as a material capable of producing realistic figurative results. This sculpture proves that realism is possible and hopefully will open people's eyes to the potential of fabric.

C

BRENNA BUSSE
UNITED STATES

Earth Elegance—Knowing She Holds Healing Green
Sculpting, stitching, beading, dyeing; clay, rayon, wool, beads, hand-dyed wool; 26 by 16 by 4 in. Photo: Petronella Vtsma

D

SUSAN DAVIS PATT
UNITED STATES

Community
Quilting, stitching, beading, screen printing, (metal is welded and bent); cotton, rayon, fabric markers, beads, steel; 31 by 37 by ¼ in.

Another collaborative piece with my husband, Stephen. This one deals with images depicting family, relationships, animals—all part of a community

A

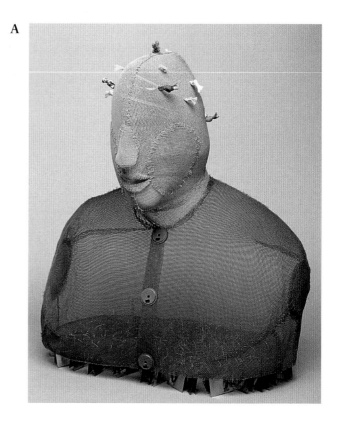

B

C

D

E

E

LENKA SUCHANEK
CANADA

Inspiration *(and detail)*
Bobbin lace; copper wire, metal
frame; 77 by 28 by 10 in.
Photo: Kenji Nagai

*As I repeat patterns created by
lacemakers 400 years ago, I
cannot refrain from thinking
about the past. During the 16th
and 17th centuries, the Old
World was stricken with famine,
disease, wars, and religious
upheavals, yet it became a cradle
for the magnificent art of
lacemaking. Renaissance ideals
are inherently present in the fine
craft of lacemaking. I believe that
is why my laceworks are about
people and their desire for love,
beauty, and harmony.*

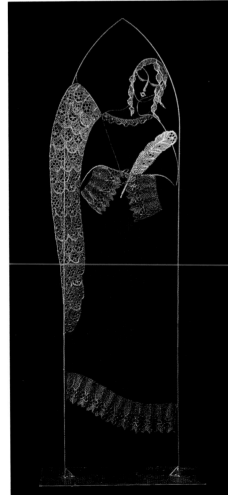

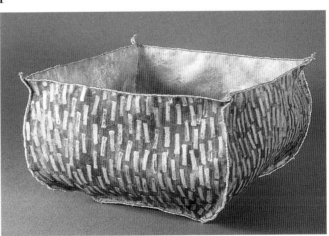

F

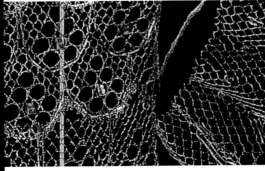

F

LEANNE M. AVELLINO
UNITED STATES

Soul Force
Hand printed, painted, sewn;
fabric, acrylic paint, printing ink;
4 by 6½ by 6½ in.

*I choose fabrics that are fluid as
well as transparent. The fabric is
painted and/or printed both
inside and out. The transparency
of the fabric is maintained
through this process so that the
viewer can be lured to the interior
of the form.*

A

CHUNGHIE LEE
KOREA

My Cup Overflows
Handmade paper, dyeing,
machine stitching; pulp,
synthetic fabric; 23 by 3 by 13
ft. Photo: Manhong Lee

B

SUSAN LEASK
ENGLAND

Poppies on the Pond
Stapling; Remembrance Day
poppies, tulle; 150 by 30 ft.

*This work was made to cover the
lake on the grounds of the
Durham Light Infantry Museum
and Art Gallery. My work is
about responding to a site, and I
wanted to find an image that
highlighted the unusual
partnership of a gallery and a
light infantry museum. I used
87,500 poppies.*

B

C

D

C

ROSA VERCAEMST
BELGIUM

Défilé
Wrapping; silk ribbons, sticks,
machine-made lace; 10 sq. ft.
Photo: Stefan Kellens

D

ELEONORA PASQUALETTI
HUNGARY

Private-Cloister
Gobelin tapestry; wool, silk,
paper; each 67 by 20 in. diameter

*My very first impression of my
Roman studies is the cloister—the
spiritual and the physical area
which is closed in a simple square.*

*On the basis of the priests' (a very
narrow class of the society)
meditation place, I tried to create
my own world and my own
cloister, which is mine and others
at the same time.*

A

A

SUGANE HARA
JAPAN

Reflections/Memory of Water
Interlaced, dyed, and painted;
rattan; 7 by 18½ by 19 ft. Photo:
Mareo Suemasa

B

MITSUKO TARUI
JAPAN

Spiral
Felting, dyeing; wool, linen, silk;
16½ by 16½ by 7 ft. Photo:
Tomohito Ishigo

B

DIVERSIONS

FRANZISKA KURTH
GERMANY

From Women, Men, Love and Frog
Gobelin, kilim tapestry; linen, wool, cotton, silk; 59 by 39 in.

I like to see life with a kind of humor and positive state of mind.
This tapestry is about what love can be.

A

LAURA GOLDBERG
UNITED STATES

Lampshade
Peyote stitch; seed beads;
12 by 8 in.

B

LINDA DOLACK
UNITED STATES

Mobile Shrine
Beading; grocery cart, beads,
charms, trinkets, candles, electric
lights; 41 by 41 by 24 in.
Photo: Tom Van Eynde

*I use humor and repetition to
allude to the endless tasks per-
formed in caring for a family.*

*Applying the beads, a mechanical
yet meditative process, took 11
months, 21 days, and I finished a
week before my 25th wedding
anniversary.*

C

MIMI HOLMES
UNITED STATES

*Migrating Flesh: Round
and Round Those Pounds
They Go*
Bead embroidery; glass beads,
wire armature, cotton, sequins,
brass bell; 16½ by 5 by 6 in.

*Now that I'm middle-aged,
pounds graft onto my body in
the most unusual places. I hope
that by making fun of this, I will
get serious about losing weight.*

A

B

C

D

E

F

D

Colleen O'Rourke
UNITED STATES

Couch

Embroidery; seed beads; 11 by 15 in. Photo: Thomas H. O'Rourke

E

Laura Leonard
UNITED STATES

Woman Who Runs With Poodles

Peyote stitch, bead embroidery; beads, wire, cotton; 19 by 15 by 15 in. Photo: Mimi Holmes

No serious art from me. Mine is about simple, everyday life...those moments of whimsy and playfulness that seemed to be everywhere when I was a girl.

F

Collis Caroline Marshall
UNITED STATES

The Best Thing Since Sliced Bread

Loom-woven, netted edging; new and antique glass beads, cotton and nylon warp and weft, found wooden object; 3½ by 4 by 2 in. Photo: Geoffrey Carr

A

CYNTHIA F. MYERBERG
UNITED STATES

The Best Prize

Xerox transfer, machine applique and piecing, hand and machine quilting; cotton; 50 by 47 in. Photo: Edward A. Petrosky

This is a tongue-in-cheek commentary of post-war values and the male-driven media propaganda that promoted the ideology of the happy homemaker.

B

BARBARA LASH
UNITED STATES

Barbie Shrine

Loom-woven and sewn; glass beads, silk, sterling silver, deer fur; 12 by 8 by 4 in

C

MARY YEAGER
UNITED STATES

Nine Female Badges of Merit

Embroidery; floss, mylar, beads; 2 in. diameter each Photo: John Haun

Viewing from left to right, the top row titles are "Pregnant," "Hot Flash," "Birth Control Pills"; middle are "Feminine Protection," "Housekeeping," "Shaving Your Legs"; and the bottom titles are "Pregnancy Test," "Lingerie," and "Measurements."

A

B
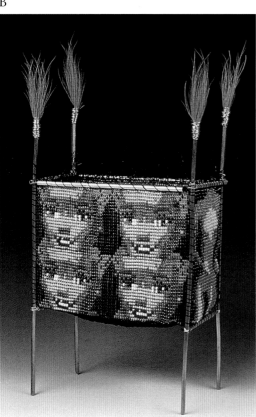

C
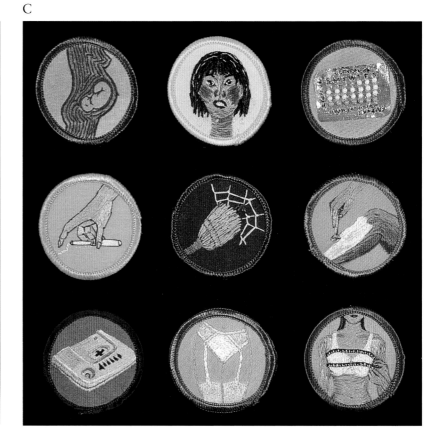

D

B. W. WATLER
UNITED STATES

Catch a Falling Star
Collage, applique, thread painting,
machine quilting; mixed fabrics;
72 by 50 in. Photo: Gerhard
Heidersberger

*The scene illustrates my impressions
of Hollywood's plastic history. Will
she fall from grace by displaying her
remarkable talents on a film director's couch? My lifetime love of
movies and puns dictated the title.*

E

VALERIE FANARJIAN
UNITED STATES

Her Majesty
Sewn assemblage; vintage sewing
ephemera, paper; 11 by 8 in.
Photo: John Lenz

F

GRETCHEN ECHOLS
UNITED STATES

*A Little Romance, A Little
Nearsightedness*
Heat transfer, applique, machine
quilting; hand dyed and commer-
cial fabrics; 31 by 45 in. Photo:
Roger Schreiber

*Sex, romance, love; it's all a tan-
gled mess. A young woman
thinks it is everything, while an
older woman knows it is only
one of the things worth having.*

A

Margaret R. Moore
UNITED STATES

Indian Corn I, II, III
Knotting; waxed linen; 10 to
11½ by 2 in. diameter

B

Joh Ricci
UNITED STATES

Four Season Pepper
Knotting, beading; nylon, seed
beads; 7½ by 2½ by 2½ in.

C

Gugger Petter
UNITED STATES

Good Dog!
Weaving; newspaper on hemp;
72 by 58 in

A

B
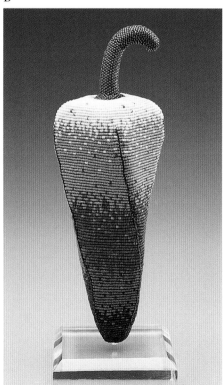

C

D

E

D

MINNAMARINA TAMMI
FINLAND

Fiona

Mixed techniques; newspaper, copper, nylon, shoes; 23½ by 39 by 39 in.

E

BERNADETTE (B.G.) BRADSHAW
UNITED STATES

You Light Up My Life

Free-motion machine embroidery; polyester thread on cotton duck; 25 by 19 in.

F

MAXINE FARKAS
UNITED STATES

The Goddess of Appropriate Attire Contemplates Her Choices

Machine pieced, hand appliqued, machine and hand quilted; found fabrics and objects; 53 by 30 in.
Photo: David Caras

I have a hard time taking some aspects of 20th-century American culture seriously. The changing moods of political correctness, the fascination with appearance, and the obsession with diet all require commentary.

F

A

B

C

D

E

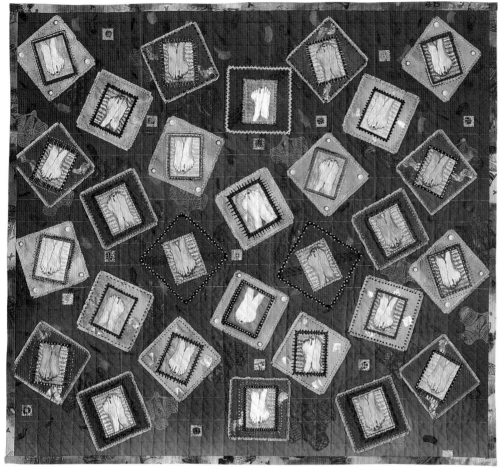

F

A

EWA KUNICZAK
SCOTLAND

Bird of Paradise
Feltmaking; merino wool

As you move when wearing the hat, the bird nods up and down; a bird on the brain or maybe just a bird brain!

B

TERESA GRAHAM SALT
UNITED STATES

Trailer Park Love
Tapestry; button silk, metallics; 8½ by 8 in

C

RENIE BRESKIN ADAMS
UNITED STATES

Sliced Banana Moon
Stitchery, painting; cotton, textile inks, pom-poms; 6¾ by 5⅝ in.

This fantasy belongs to the child who is saying, "Stop, this is my world; you can't come in."

D

ANNE McGINN
UNITED STATES

Blizzard the Lizard
Tapestry, eccentric wefts; cotton; 16¼ by 12½ in. Photo: Michael Scarpelli

This is an illustration from a collection of poems written for and with Emily, who was four at the time. Blizzard is our moniker for a chameleon we spied sunbathing on a red Adirondack chair.

E

WENDY C. HUHN
UNITED STATES

48 Feet
Emulsion and solvent transfer, airbrushing, applique, painting, drawing; Polaroid image, silk, mirrors; 43 by 48 in. Photo: David Loveall Photography

This is an ode to my feet. I have the world's worst and have never been able to wear high heels.

F

RUTH MANNING
UNITED STATES

Tiptoe Waitress
Handwoven tapestry; wool, cotton; 10 by 11 in. Photo: Richard Margolis

Entering the work force after a hiatus of 20 years was challenging, to say the least, and waiting tables can be grueling work. This said, I am struck by the lightheartedness and camaraderie that rises above it all. During a slow time, a waitress tiptoed around the room, deliberately placing each foot on a diamond of the rug pattern.

I'm still hoping for imminent retirement, with the cups of coffee served to me instead.

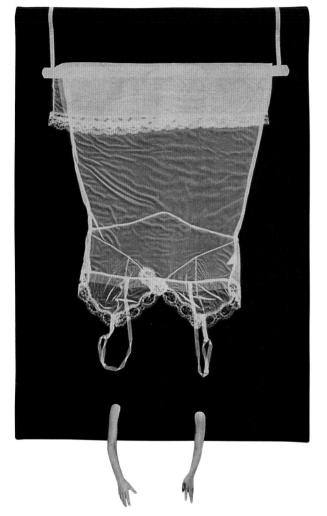

E

A

CAROL ADLEMAN
UNITED STATES

Slip
Cyanotype, color Xerox; cotton;
45 by 28 in.

B

MARIANNE FLENNIKEN
UNITED STATES

Wedding Gown
Machine sewn, pop riveted; aluminum mesh Photo: Jacqueline
Rogers

*The quilting tradition makes silk
purses out of sows' ears. I hope
this piece reflects that tradition
and the resourcefulness, artistry,
and strength of women.*

C

JEAN HICKS
UNITED STATES

Sushi Cocktail Hat
Felting, millinery techniques;
merino wool, kimono silk, chopsticks Photo: Jan Cook

D

CAROLA FARTHING
UNITED STATES

Diet Dreams
Cutting, sewing; cottage cheese
containers, candy bar wrappers,
screen cloth Photo: Gugger Petter

You can't judge a vest by its cover!

E

PATTY GALLAGHER
UNITED STATES

Patty! Set the Table!
Sewing, construction; turntable
umbrella, silk flowers, sound
effect of crickets Photo: Tom
Little

F

MARTINE CAILLON-
HOUSE
UNITED STATES

*Do Not Disturb My
Garden Fairies*
Applique, embroidery, beading,
quilting, trapunto, macrame;
hand-dyed cotton, silk, beads; 34
by 49 in. Photo: Carlynn Tucker

*This is my view of the magical
world, inspired in part by
Botticelli's painting, La Primavera,
and the Disney cartoon, Fantasia.*

F

A

EMILY PARSON
UNITED STATES

Hot Line

Reverse and direct appliqued, machine quilted; hand-dyed and -painted cotton; 46 by 48 in.

I collect household objects from the 1950s and '60s. The rotary dial telephone is becoming obsolete in the age of cellular and portable and I wanted to honor it.

B

CAROL DRUMMOND
UNITED STATES

Let the Good Times Roll

Machine applique, hand quilting; commercial fabric, buttons; 23 by 25 in. Photo: Rick Drummond

C

HOOP
UNITED STATES

Heli-Hoop

Painting, applied synthetic fur

I love to take off in the Heli-Hoop and survey the art world in my fiber art flying machine.

A

B

C

Paper and Felt

Dabney Hammer
UNITED STATES

October Pillow
Felting, stitching, weaving; merino wool, mohair, silk;
19 by 18 by 6½ in. Photo: Chip Clark

A

Carol Owen
UNITED STATES

Largo

Papermaking, assembling, collage; handmade paper, found objects; 18 by 15 by 7 in. Photo: Jerry Blow

B

Patricia Zobel Canaday
UNITED STATES

Caught

Papermaking; handmade paper, flax, wood; 29 by 12 by 21 in. Photo Chip Belden

For me, the boat means fragility. There is a fine line between boat and water, life and death.

C

Karen Simmons
UNITED STATES

Nest #5

Papermaking; cattail leaves, abaca, honeysuckle vine, waxed linen, dye; 28 by 10 by 10 in. Photo: Margot Geist

A

C

B

D

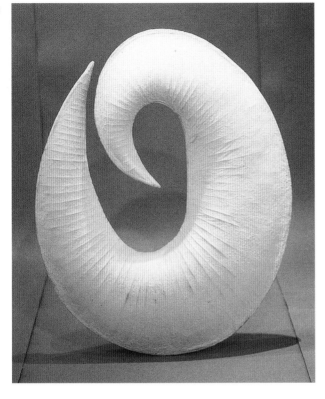

D

KYUNGAE JEON
KOREA

Untitled

Papermaking, forming; handmade
and cast paper, armature; 38 by
31 by 8 in.

E

SANDY WEBSTER
UNITED STATES

Reference (and detail)

Papermaking, assembling; hay,
wood, seeds, tobacco, herbs,
manure; 14 by 10 by 18 in.

*The piece represents my
connection to the men in the
Southern rural community where
I live.*

E

A

Nicole Dextras
CANADA

Barbara, Wing Siu and Andy
Papermaking, Xerox transfer;
cast handmade paper, flax,
pigments, silk, acrylic medium;
84 by 60 by 12 in.

B

Pamela Sullivan
UNITED STATES

Perspective
Papermaking, stamping, collage,
hand and machine embroidery;
handmade paper, copper leaf; 7½
by 34 in. Photo: Clifford Wheeler

A

B

C

C

NAN GOSS
UNITED STATES

Blue Beech Leaves
Papermaking, painting, hand and
machine stitching; handmade
paper, copper, glass and metal
beads, twig, leaves; 11½ by 22in.
Photo: Ken Wagner

D

CAS HOLMES
ENGLAND

Tea and Tales
Papermaking, dye painting and
printing, stitching, quilting;
handmade paper, teabags, dye,
found objects; 47 by 47 in.

*The piece was made shortly after
my grandmother, a Romany,
died.*

D

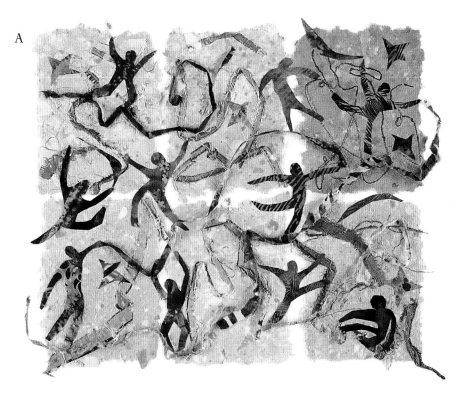

A

A
MARY BETH SCHWARTZENBERGER
UNITED STATES

Joie de Vie
Papermaking, cutting, collage; handmade paper, silk, cotton; 23½ by 20½ in.
Photo: Paul Moshay

Creating collage answers my frustration for spontaneity after 20 years of weaving.

B
SUSAN CUTTS
ENGLAND

Stiletto
Papermaking; handmade, sculpted paper; each 7 by 4 by 10 in. Photo: Patrick Gorman

I am captivated by the magic of shoes. They are necessary, seductive, sculptural, and a source of limitless inspiration.

C
MARIA DIDUCH
THE NETHERLANDS

Reminiscence
Papermaking; handmade paper, silk, cotton; 57 by 35 by 8 cm.
Photo: Michael Mulder

C

B

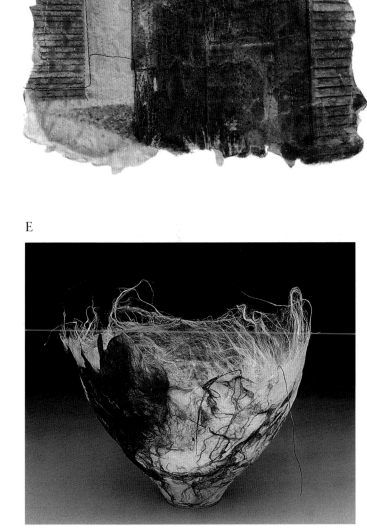

D

CAROL HOLLAND
ENGLAND

Net Sheds & Chapel

Papermaking, cyanotype and Van Dyke brownprint, machine stitching; handmade paper, silk; 16 by 11 in.

The weatherboard structures were built in Tudor times to dry fishing nets. The fishermen's chapel, now deconsecrated and a museum, was built in 1854.

E

ANDREA TUCKER-HODY
UNITED STATES

Medium Fiber Vessel

Papermaking; handmade paper, kozo; 18 by 7 by 4½ in. Photo: George Post

F

INGRID THOMAS HOOKER
UNITED STATES

Collected Paths II

Papermaking; handmade, pigmented, and cast paper; 39 by 31 in.

The Rappites founded a utopian community, Harmony, Indiana, along the banks of the Wabash River. That's where I first experienced a labyrinth.

F

A

LEANDRA SPANGLER
UNITED STATES

Out of Ireland
Papermaking, collage; cast and
embossed handmade paper,
graphite; 8 by 14 in. Diameter
Photo: Helios Studio

*Instead of using graphite to make
linear marks, I use it to enhance
and define the surface quality of
my handmade paper.*

B

CLAUDIA LEE
UNITED STATES

Three Lamps
Papermaking, stitching, dyeing;
kozo, leaves, twigs, indigo, linen;
each 6 by 4 by 4 in. Photo:
Christy Shivell

C

JOCELYNE GAUDREAU
CANADA

Pouces tapis dans les nattes
Papermaking, painting,
assembling; handmade paper,
acrylic paint; 24 by 36 by 2 in.

*The piece salutes the hands that
braid, the hands that participate
so much in the making of an
object that they become a part
of it.*

A

B

C

D

D

Karen Simmons
UNITED STATES

Shrine
Papermaking, construction;
narcissus, abaca, honeysuckle
vine, salt cedar, waxed linen,
dye, bone beads; 12 by 17 by 24
in. Photo: Margot Geist

*After many years as a
production weaver, I appreciate
the spontaneity of working with
paper and other natural
elements.*

E

Genie Shenk
UNITED STATES

Wordbook (and detail)
Papermaking, construction; kozo,
mica, laserprint; each 30 by 25 in.

*This is about the dual nature of
language, the power of words to
conceal as well as reveal. The
interplay of transparency and
opacity is crucial to the concept.*

E

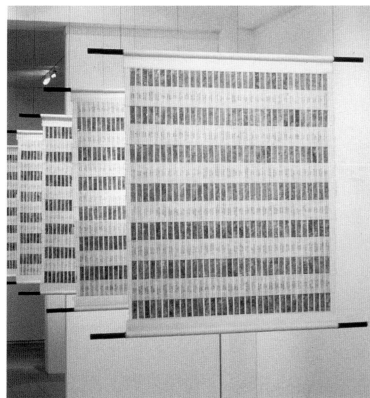

A

B

C

D

E

F

A

SUSAN LEOPOLD
CANADA

Bless This House
Papermaking; handmade paper,
post-consumer goods; 11 by 8½
in. Photo: See Spot Run

B

SUSAN LEOPOLD
CANADA

World Hunger
Papermaking; handmade paper,
post-consumer goods; 11 by 8 in.
Photo: See Spot Run

C

KIM GOURLAY
SCOTLAND

St. Pierre des Champs
Felting, hand and machine
stitching, painting,
collage; wool, linen, acrylic
medium; 15 by 29 in.
Photo: Alex Gunn

*This work evolved from
impressions of the surrounding
landscape of St. Pierre des
Champs, a small village in the
south of France.*

D

JERLYN CABA
UNITED STATES

Coat of Rules
Papermaking, photo transfer;
handmade and cast paper, gold
foil; 17 by 14 in.

E

LORE LINDENFELD
UNITED STATES

Flight
Stitching, drawing; Japanese
paper, polyester, mylar; 9 by 9 by
3 in. Photo: D. James Dee

*I am intrigued with the potential
of transforming and reinventing
images of natural forms by
combining the real with the
imagined.*

F

CAROLYN PRINCE
BATCHELOR
UNITED STATES

Lizard Vest
Painting, sewing; paper, paint,
thread; 18 by 15 in.
Photo: Mark Middleton

*I paint sheets of paper, tear them,
and roll them to form beads.
Each bead is sewn by hand to a
reinforced paper shape that
represents an imaginary garment.*

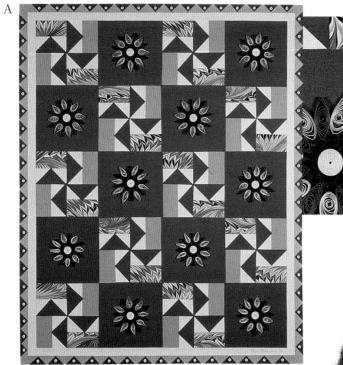

A

B

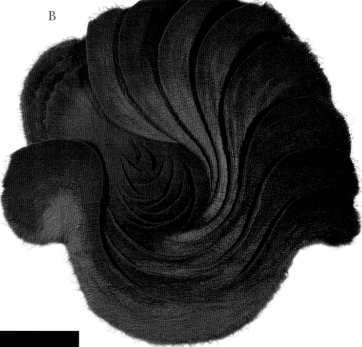

C

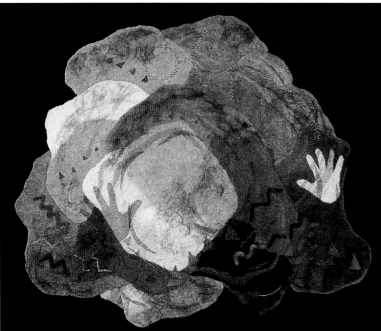

D

A

KAREN MOSKOWITZ
UNITED STATES

Limantour (and detail)
Quilling, collage; paper, mat
board; 23 by 18½ in. Photo:
Gugger Petter

B

YUKIKO NISHIOKA
UNITED STATES

Dangerous Beauty: Predator
Felting; wool; 43 by 47 in.

C

PATRICIA SPARK
UNITED STATES

Maelstrom: Time's Lair
Felting, beading, stitching,
applique; merino wool, nylon, silk
paper, glass beads; 36 by 43 in.

D

VIBEKE S. PEDERSEN
UNITED STATES

Young Man
Felting; dyed wool; 16 by 12½ in.

E

JOYCE KING
UNITED STATES

*Movement Without
Words (and detail)*
Felting, embroidery; wool, gold
thread; 16 by 20 in.

E

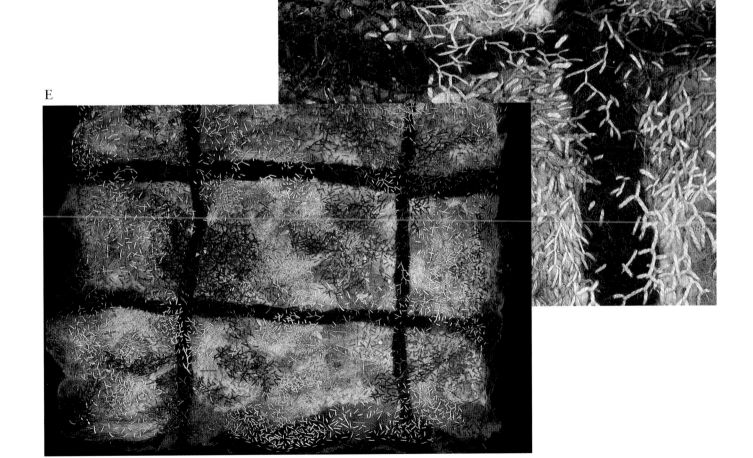

A

Molly R.-M. Fowler
UNITED STATES

Salubrious Exploration
Felting, knotless netting; wool,
mohair, silk; 70 by 24 by 4 in.

*This was commissioned by an
artist/writer who makes
discoveries while achieving well
being, balance, and tranquility.
Any swimmer can understand
this phenomenon.*

B

Jeannie Fierce
UNITED STATES

Sweet Loraine
Felting, cutting; wool, mohair
yarn; 39 by 29 in.

A

B

C

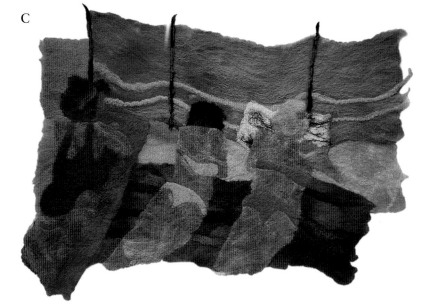

C

CLARE DIPROSE
ENGLAND

Cornwall I - Bathers
Felting; dyed merino wool; 24 by 36 in.

D

LESLIE MACNEIL
UNITED STATES

Elements Flight
Felting, dyeing, stitching; wool; 52 by 86 in. Photo: Andrew Edgar

The concept behind the piece reflects an almost whirling dervish aspect of my life as a self-employed, full time artist. Sometimes I feel as if I am flying through life; other times, as if I have been dropped, like Dorothy, into my own personal Oz.

D

E

E

CECILIA VOSS EAGER
UNITED STATES

Lily, Family Dog
Felting, sewing; wool; 22½ by 40 in.

Everyone in the family has a different pet name for our border collie.

A

A

RENEE HARRIS
UNITED STATES

Three Red Bushes *(and detail)*
Felting, embroidery; hand-dyed
wool, cotton thread; 9½ by 13½
in. Photo: C. W. Schauer

B

STEPHANIE GILBERT
ENGLAND

*The Story of Adam
and Eve* *(and detail)*
Felting, embroidery; hand-dyed
felt, beads; 39 by 32 in.

B

SURFACE DESIGN

SHIIKO ALEXANDER
UNITED STATES

Kimono USA

Heat transfer, screen printed, collaged, painted; silk, paper,
gold leaf, wood, found objects; 36 by 24 by 3 in.

*In Tokyo, where I grew up, contradictions are everywhere:
Western and Eastern, old and new, rustic and refined. I am attracted to
and fascinated by materials left behind in a changing world.*

A

ANN SCHROEDER
UNITED STATES

Natural Forces #2
Painted, machine pieced and
quilted; cotton, canvas, textile
inks, acrylic paint; 44 by 42½ in.
Photo: David Caras

B

ASTRID HILGER BENNETT
UNITED STATES

India Cafe
Painted, screen printed, monoprinted, machine quilted; cotton,
fiber reactive dye; 54 by 78 in.
Photo: Mark Tade

*The "Handwork" series pays
homage to the unseen hand in the
events of artists' lives; the hand,
too, that binds friendships among
us. The color palette was inspired
by many Friday lunches shared
with an artist friend at the India
Cafe in Iowa City, Iowa.*

C

TERESA PASCHKE
UNITED STATES

Allotment
Starch resist, frottage, dyed,
embroidered; canvas, graphite,
gel medium; 55 by 90 in.

*From the "Human Activity"
series, the work reflects my interest in the marks and impressions
we leave behind as we live our
lives.*

D

ERIKA CARTER
UNITED STATES

Flow VI
Painted, machine appliqued,
hand and machine quilted; cotton, silk organza; 46 by 38½ in.
Photo: Howard Carter

*The emphasis in my current
work is on the painted surface
versus directing the work
through construction methods.*

E

JANE DUNNEWOLD
UNITED STATES

Untitled Yardage (detail)
Dyed, overdyed, reverse printed;
rayon/silk velvet; 54 by 54 in.

*I am currently working on
lengths of yardage as works of
art in and of themselves, with no
eye toward "function."*

A

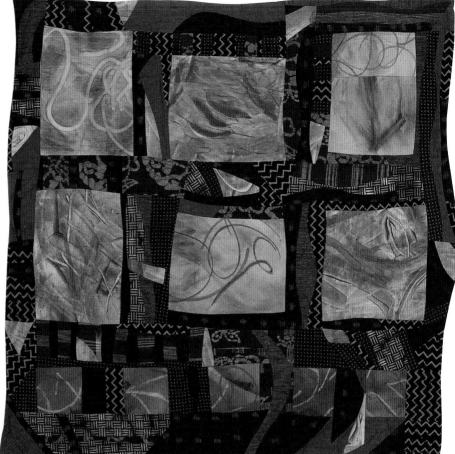

B

C

D

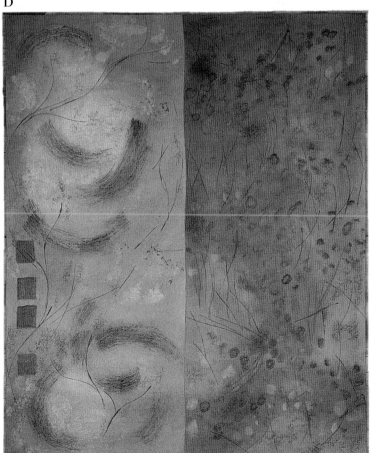

E

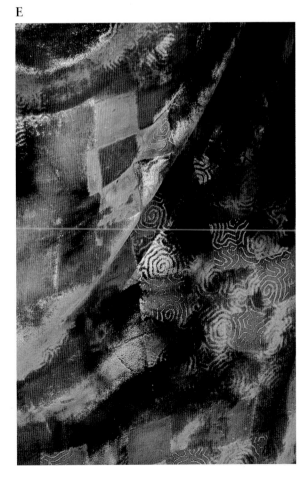

A

PATRICIA KENNEDY-ZAFRED
UNITED STATES

The Promise #2

Photo transfer, machine pieced and quilted; cotton, vinyl, acetate; 21 by 24 in. Photo: Peter Shefler

B

JOANNE WOLL
UNITED STATES

Couch Paintings—Mix or Match

Photo transfer, monoprint, stamped, hand and machine stitched; cotton, textile paint; 25 by 23 in. Photo: Master Slide

This piece came about when my daughter wanted a painting to match her couch. The small paintings are photocopies of my own paintings attached to the piece with VELCRO® so they can be moved about to mix or match the couches.

A

B

C

D

E

C

MARY LOU PEPE
UNITED STATES

The Trophy - Child's Play

Photo transfer, machine pieced, beaded, and quilted; China silk, polyester lace bra, beads, pearls; 47 by 32 in. Photo: Peter F. Pepe

The concept is based on Tic Tac Toe. I used a mirror image of a bra to create the Xs, and a single heart represents the O. Remembering how important the size of my bra was to me as a teenager, I integrated a poem within the piece.

D

LINDA PINHAY
CANADA

St. Alban's

Screen printed (polychromatic); cotton, fiber reactive dye; 28 by 36 in.

St. Alban's is a church in the north of England where I attended Sunday school.

E

PATRICIA KENNEDY-ZAFRED
UNITED STATES

Veiled Intentions

Screen printed, painted, machine pieced and quilted; cotton, organza, spray and oil paint; 30 by 28 in. Photo: Peter Shefler

My current work uses the human face in an attempt to tell a story, create a memory, or evoke an emotion. The viewer's interpretation is therefore an integral part of the success of the work.

A

B

A

DENISE TALLON HAVLAN
UNITED STATES

Nocturnal Embrace

Painted, fused, machine embroidered and quilted; cotton, textile paint and ink; 50½ by 49½ in.

On this piece, I concentrated on the negative space and was inspired by my love for black cats, which seem to find their way into my life!

B

MIRIAM NATHAN-ROBERTS
UNITED STATES

Fiber Dance

Airbrushed, machine pieced, appliqued, and quilted; hand-dyed fabric; 57 by 61 in.

I have been interested in structure and illusions of depth all my life. I have no real depth perception because my eyes don't achieve fusion (one is near-sighted and the other is far-sighted). I designed this quilt three years before I made it because it took that long for me to figure out how to make it and to learn to airbrush.

C

ROXANA BARTLETT
UNITED STATES

If Recollecting Were Forgetting

Painted, dyed, pieced, appliqued; cotton, Procion dye, acrylic paint; 69 by 69 in. Photo: Ken Sanville

C

D

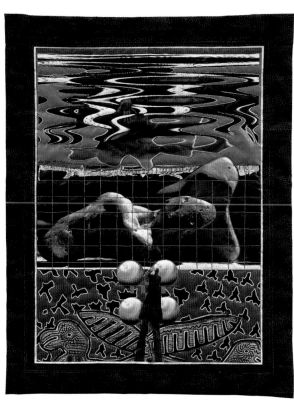

F

D

JEAN L. KARES
CANADA

Every Road Leads Home
Screen printed; cotton, pigments, metallic cord, metal leaf; 40 by 29 in.

E

ARLE SKLAR-WEINSTEIN
UNITED STATES

Message from Another Domain
Digital print transfer, machine pieced, quilted, and embroidered; satin, cotton; 24 by 18¾ in. Photo: D. James Dee

In this work from the "Mola" series, I have taken the form of the double eagle from an old faded mola in my collection. The two-way vision of that image is a perfect metaphor for much of my life. It is barely in the picture within a hot subterranean area. The shadow figure is both the receiver and the source of the message.

F

NANCY FORREST
UNITED STATES

A Room With a View
Airbrushed, pieced, appliqued, quilted; airbrush-dyed cotton; 72 by 56 in. Photo: Mark Frey

This quilt is about different layers of reality that coexist in time and space. In the humblest of rooms, at a seemingly mundane moment, I suspect that something very profound and sacred is taking place—if we only had the eyes to see it.

A

Jacqueline Treloar
CANADA

Kirsten and Arianne
Stencilled, painted; nylon; 102 by
135 in. Collection of Tim
Dawson, Toronto

B

Leslie Nobler Farber
UNITED STATES

Origami Heroes
Photography, computer manipulation, collaged, stitched, beaded;
fabric, paper, foil, computer
printouts, pastels, beads; 31 by
28 in. Photo: Howard Nathenson

*I am exploring the function of
the machine versus the hand.
While much of the visual work
takes place efficiently on my
Macintosh, the labor of the piece
is slowly accomplished by hand.*

C

Mara Kali
UNITED STATES

Trans.
Painted, stitched, waxed; chiffon,
graphite; 48 by 60 in. Photo:
CSU Photographic Services

Trans. *relates to transparent,
translucent, and transient, and
deals with my feelings during*
marriage and divorce. This piece
is about women not being seen
or heard, about being an object,
about carrying our wounds in
our bodies, and ultimately about
recognizing this and approaching
healing.

A

C

B

D

Lee Lapthorne
ENGLAND

Man

Photo transfer, dyed, machine embroidered; Procion dye, wax paper; 10 by 8 in.

E

Carolyn A. Dahl
UNITED STATES

Vision Lost, Visions Gained

Relief print, dyed, collaged; fabric, paper, photocopies; 17 by 28 in. Photo: Maria Davila

I knew I was grieving deeply for the clear vision I lost during a retinal detachment when I started to save dying flowers. Placing them in a telephone book, I'd press the last bit of life out until their veins laid down on the paper like threads. When I began to see beauty and inspiration in their flattened, lifeless forms, I knew I was on my way to emotional healing.

F

Nadine Miller
UNITED STATES

Muse

Heat transfer, construction; original photographs, cotton; each 72 by 38 in.

My work represents a 17-year-old love affair with the photocopier.

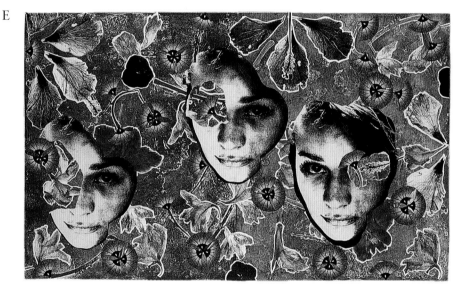

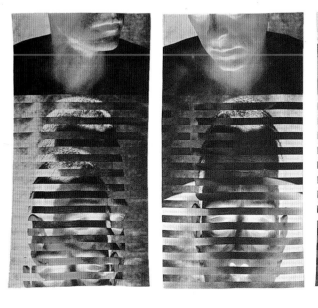

A

B

C

A

ANN BELLINGER
HARTLEY
UNITED STATES

Wings
Photo transfer, painted, collaged,
sewn; fabric, paper, acrylic paint;
15 by 11 in.

B

JOAN SCHULZE
UNITED STATES

Fin de Siècle
Printed, painted, quilted, photo
transfer; silk, cotton, paper; 51
by 51 in. Photo: Sharon
Risedorph

*Like everyone else, I have been
thinking about 2001. Here's my
millennium effort.*

C

LAUREN ROSENBLUM
UNITED STATES

Waiting
Silkscreened, block stamped,
hand quilted; hand-dyed cotton;
82 by 70 in. Photo: D. James Dee

Waiting *is about taking control
and realizing the power of
choice.*

D

D

AKEMI NAKANO COHN
UNITED STATES

Assimilation

Rice paste resist, katazome, stamped, interlaced, stitched; silk; 43 by 45 in. Photo: Garry Henderson

Interlacing has emerged as an important process in my work. I print two fabrics, applying traditional rice paste resist techniques. One is printed in English; the other in Japanese. I cut them in strips and interlace them.

E

RACHEL BRUMER
UNITED STATES

Long Associations

Brownprint, silkscreened, stamped, stitched, pieced, appliqued; hand-dyed and commercial cotton, linen, silk; 69 by 78 in. Photo: Mark Frey

E

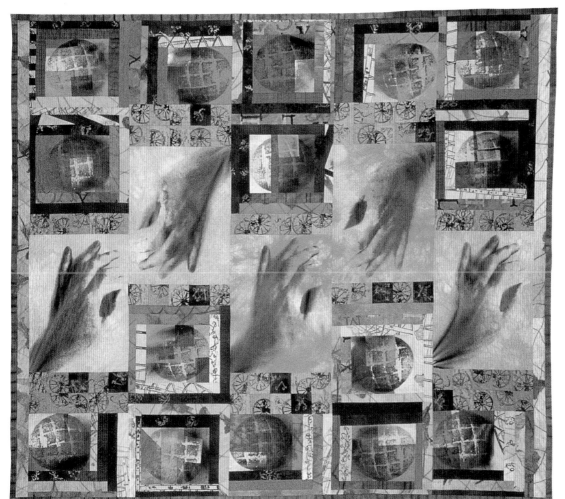

A

Barbara Schulman
UNITED STATES

Contemporary Ego-Systems
Painted, printed, stitched, woven;
cotton, 35mm slides, pen points,
blades, found objects; 36 by 32
in. Photo: Robert Walch

*This autobiographical work is
constructed from personal
objects, woven fragments, and
artist's tools. I focus on the con-
tradiction between the soft/secure
actuality of a quilt and the dan-
gerous/humorous aspects of my
life as an artist. The X-Acto
blades and pen points refer to the
perils of the art world and the
dangers of certain artworks.*

B

Erma Martin Yost
UNITED STATES

Rainbow Seekers
Solargram, machine appliqued
and embroidered; cotton,
organza; 23 by 31 in. Photo:
courtesy of NOHO Gallery,
New York

A

B

C

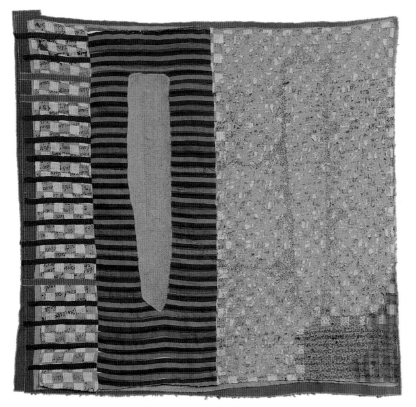

D

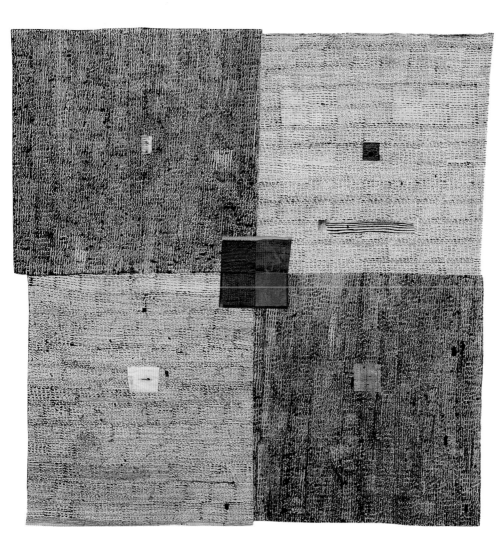

C

SONDRA L. DORN
UNITED STATES

Projection: Number One
Screen printed, discharge painted, dyed, appliqued, embroidered; linen, silk, cotton; 36½ by 36 in. Photo: Robert Chiarito

I am focusing on using complex arrangements of color, pattern, texture, and line and exploring how these elements relate to one another.

D

DOROTHY CALDWELL
CANADA

Four Patch: Hay/Wheat/Rye/Barley
Wax resist and discharge dyed, stitched, quilted (by Grace Foxton, Lydia Kelder, Ruth Lamont, Evelyn Martn); cotton; 96 by 98 in.
Photo: Thomas Moore

This piece came out of a study of early Canadian quilts. I related the simplest quilt configuration, the "four patch," to the four fields of my farm. It was quilted by a group of women whose fine, even stitching contrasts with my large, clunky stitches, forming a connection in the piece to the practices of traditional quiltmaking.

A

B

C

A

ETHEL SHULAM
UNITED STATES

Big Catch Dream
Painted, dyed, fused, machine
embroidered, quilted, and
appliquéd; cotton, mylar, feath-
ers; 51½ by 40½ in.
Photo: David Caras

B

M. JOAN LINTAULT
UNITED STATES

Give Us This Day
Dyed, printed, painted,
appliquéd, quilted; machine lace,
commercial fabric, beads; 69 by
63 in. Photo: Dan Overturf

*A still life is an indoor represen-
tation of paradise. This piece
shows the abundance of the
earth—our paradise.*

C

RACHEL LAWRENCE
EDWARDS
UNITED STATES

Cultivating Memories
Photo transfer, airbrushed, cro-
cheted, beaded, machine embroidered; cotton, silk, foil beads,
antique glasses; 62 by 45 in.
Photo: J. Scott Schrader

D

HYANGSOOK PARK
KOREA

Meditation '95
Screen printed, wax resist dyed;
silk; 76 by 48 in.

E

CLARE VERSTEGEN
UNITED STATES

Wait a Minute
Screen printed; canvas, pigments;
76 by 24 in.

*Ready or not, the bell of a
kitchen timer measures a pre-
scribed period that ends the tick-
ing of time. In* Wait a Minute, *I
want to portray a quiet quality of
rhythm and balance, where
worry does not overtake, but
creeps slowly into the cadence of
the pattern.*

D

E

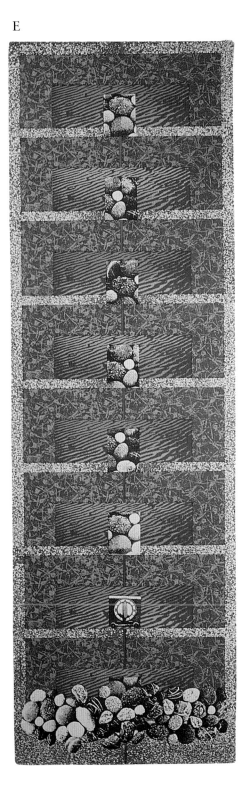

A

DANA BOUSSARD
UNITED STATES

Marksman 1st Class
Painted, cut, appliqued; cotton velvet, fabric paint; 55 by 66 in.
Photo: Kurt Wilson

B

CLARE FRANCES SMITH
NEW ZEALAND

Paramecium Dreams
Machine pieced and quilted, hand appliqued; sprayed, hand-dyed, and screen printed cotton; 41 by 36½ in.
Photo: Howard Williams

C

CLARE FRANCES SMITH
NEW ZEALAND

Sleeping with the Enemy
Dyed, sprayed, painted, printed, appliqued, pieced, quilted; cotton; 45½ by 50 in. Photo: Gilbert van Reenen

As an allergy sufferer, I sometimes wonder why I make quilts; they're just homes for dust mites!

A

B

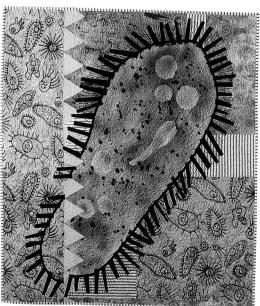

C

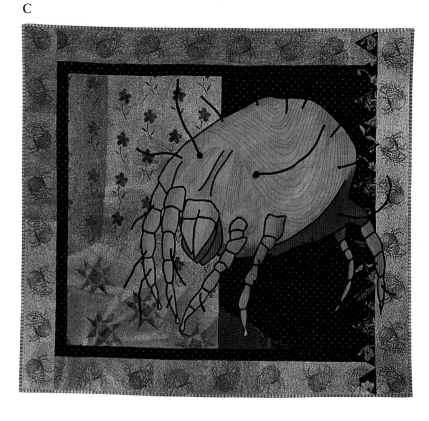

D

E

F

D

**VICTORIA RABINOWE**
UNITED STATES

Dreamboat: a Self-Portrait
Painted; silk, fiber reactive dye;
34 by 36 in. Photo: Ray Medina

E

HEATHER ALLEN
UNITED STATES

32 Warwick
Painted, silkscreen printed, rice
paste resist, discharge dyed,
monoprinted; cotton, textile ink,
beads; 75 by 36 in.
Photo: Tim Barnwell

F

MICHALENE GROSHEK
UNITED STATES

Night Walks
Screen printed, painted,
appliqued, beaded; felted wool,
canvas, beads; 33 by 24 in.
Photo: Bill Lemke

*This piece (from the "North
Lake" series) embraces the concept of total freedom to walk
about at night in a rural environment.*

A

LUCY A. JAHNS
UNITED STATES

Rainbow Forest

Dyed, machine appliqued and embroidered; fabric, canvas; 36½ by 54 in.

Rainbow Forest *was inspired by one of my daughter Emily's drawings.*

B

BETSY STERLING BENJAMIN
JAPAN

Eastern Portal—Spain

Roketsu-zome, wax resist, stitched, discharge dyed, stencilled; silk, gold powder; 48½ by 19 in. Photo: Y. Tange

C

BERNIE ROWELL
UNITED STATES

For the Tribe of One-Breasted Women

Painted, fused, appliqued, collaged, machine embroidered; fabric, leather, vinyl, beads; 60 by 37 in. Photo: David Luttrell

A

C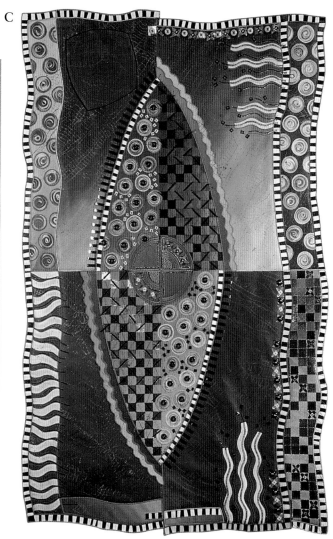

B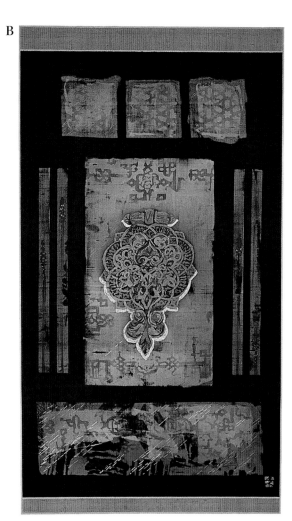

D

F

E

D

SOON SIL PARK
UNITED STATES

Memento
Painted, stencilled; guache, gold powder; 12 by 10 in.

E

JAN JANAS
UNITED STATES

Gaia: Goddess of Earth
Painted, stamped, stencilled; silk broadcloth, French dye, acrylic paint; 72 by 36 in.

This is a subjective, archetypal image that was inspired by a passage in Cloete's book, The Turning Wheels: *"Today is the child of yesterday and the mother of tomorrow. Tomorrow is already in her womb striving to be free."*

F

CHRISTI TEASLEY
UNITED STATES

Berry Dance
Chemical and potato dextrin resist, stitched; metallic/silk organza, velvet, linen, rust; 44 by 20 in. Photo: Jim Ann Howard

This work can be viewed as analogous to memory—decomposing fragments of recollections, with lapses, gaps, and holes, faded and fading, incomplete but constantly overlaid by the newer, more active, bright and colorful collections of the most recent past.

A

A

Vita Marie Lovett
UNITED STATES

Butterfly Hinge

Thread painted, quilted; canvas, cotton, acrylic paint; 15¼ by 20¾ in. Photo: Hambrick's Photography

While driving along a country road in Georgia, I came upon this old barn, once painted red. Large rusted hinges hold the splitting doors in place. This is from my "Primitive Door" series.

B

Linda MacDonald
UNITED STATES

Portrait of J. Robert Oppenheimer

Airbrushed, painted, dyed, quilted; cotton; 49 by 43 in. Photo: Carina Woolrich

Fifty years had passed since the first atom bomb was created. I wanted to recognize that as well as the man who was the director of the Trinity Project.

C

Robin Schwalb
UNITED STATES

Izba

Photo screen printed, stencilled, machine pieced, hand appliqued and quilted; commercial fabric, fabric paint; 71 by 48 in. Photo: Karen Bell

An izba is a Russian peasant's wooden house, often decorated with elaborate fretwork. For Russians, an izba conjures the same kind of sentimental associations that a log cabin does for Americans. The text that stretches across the weathered "wall posters" is from Gogol's Dead Souls *and is about the compelling emotional pull of this troubled and complex land.*

A

C

B

D

D

SUSAN BRANDEIS
UNITED STATES

Windows #14
Dyed, screen printed, reverse appliqued, stitched, beaded; cotton, seed beads; 13½ by 18¼ in.
Photo: Marc Brandeis

The works in the "Windows" series are based on the shifting patterns of light through my kitchen window shutters.

E

BETH P. GILBERT
UNITED STATES

Lest We Forget
Photo transfer, painted, stamped, stencilled, pieced, appliqued, machine embroidered and quilted; cotton; 77 by 67 in.
Photo: Ken Wagner

The three areas of text are: a) a description of the slaughter of 33,000 Jews at Babi Yar in the Ukraine; b) an account of the Warsaw Ghetto uprising; and c) a poem by a 12-year-old girl who perished in Auschwitz.

E

A

B

C

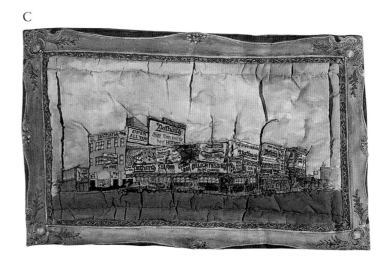

D

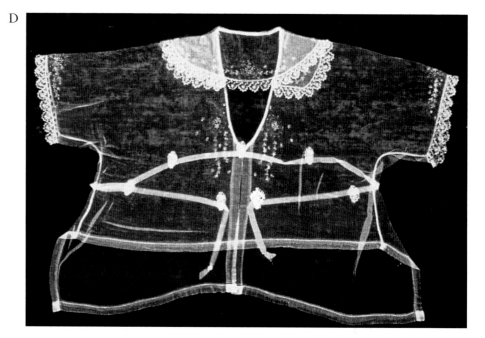

A

ROSEMARY BARILE
UNITED STATES

Tree Posture
Solvent transfer, block printed,
stitched; silk organza, metallic
pencil, seeds, mylar; 36½ by 21½
in. Photo: Richard Nicol

B

JACQUES PETE
FRANCE

The Head Somewhere Else
Batik; silk; 15 by 18 in.

E

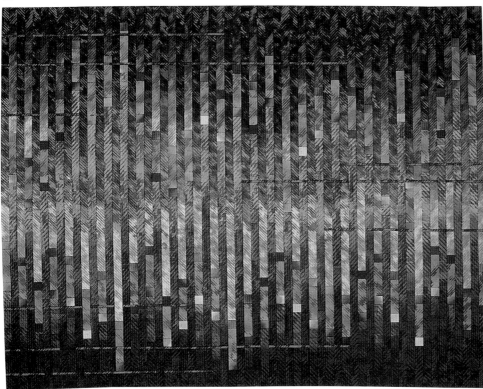

F

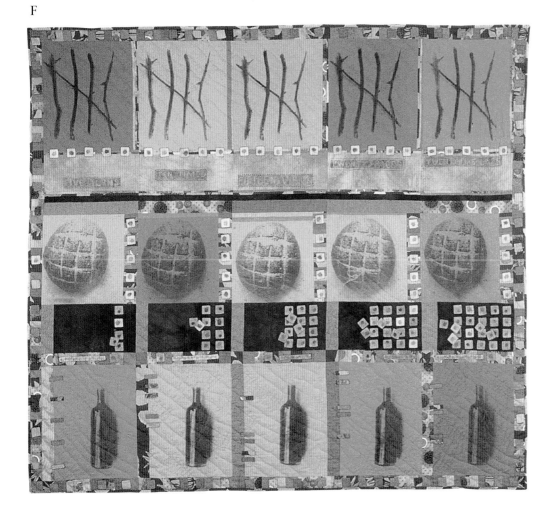

C

LOUISE FISCHER COZZI
UNITED STATES

Nathan's

Photo transfer and collage,
painted, quilted; cotton, fabric
paint; 9¾ by 15 by in.

*This piece is one of a series on
the architecture of Brooklyn, my
hometown by birth and choice.*

D

CAROL ADLEMAN
UNITED STATES

The Bedjacket

Cyanotype, embroidery; cotton;
25 by 36 in.

*I really love the shape and the
marvelous cut of this very old bedjacket. It is sheer enough to let the
light through—all the way through
to its skeleton, the bare bones!*

E

CHRISTINE L. ZOLLER
UNITED STATES

Classical Compliments

Screen printed; cotton, textile
pigments; 48 by 56 in.
Photo: Catherine Walker

F

RACHEL BRUMER
UNITED STATES

Keeping Track

Brownprint, stained, machine
pieced, hand quilted, embroidery;
hand-dyed and commercial cotton;
56 by 62 in. Photo: Mark Frey

*I have had three nonverbal
careers. My creative life began as
a dancer and choreographer. After
working for 15 years, I retired.
My second career was as a sign-
language interpreter. For the past
10 years, I've been making art
quilts. I am committed to the idea
of a visual language and to developing a personal vocabulary of
visual images.*

A

AMIE ADELMAN
UNITED STATES

Controlling Hand
Screen printed, painted, dyed; canvas, fiber reactive dye; 92½ by 68 in. Photo: Jon Blumb

Two red clock hands isolated from others draw the viewer's attention to the hour at which I was born. Time defines the moments in one's life, but also reminds us of the constraints it imposes.

B

NANCY N. ERICKSON
UNITED STATES

Confined
Painted, appliqued, sewn; satin, cotton, fabric paint; 57 by 59 in.

C

MARTHA DESPOSITO
UNITED STATES

Held Hostage
Xerox transfers, painted, collaged, stamped; fabric, pastels, acrylic paint; 47 by 42 in. Photo: Harry Edelman

This work was created in reaction to my forced move to Pittsburgh, Pennsylvania in 1994. It reflects my involvement with the renovations of an old house that took six months to complete.

D

JANE DUNNEWOLD
UNITED STATES

Untitled Yardage (detail)
Screen printed; cotton, pigment, foil; 54 by 144 in.

E

LESLEY RICHMOND
CANADA

Leaf Skeleton
Devoré, dyed, burned, beaded, machine embroidered; silk/rayon velvet, silk/rayon charmeuse; 30 by 25 in.

I wanted to comment on the seasonal growth and decay of plant structures—on their vulnerability in a crowded world, and on the realization that even decay has its own fragile beauty.

A

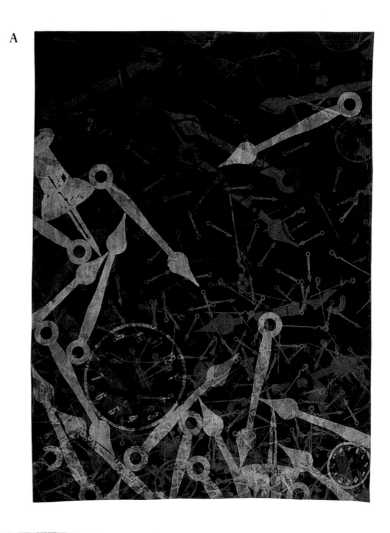

B

C

D

E

A

GRETCHEN ECHOLS
UNITED STATES

The Still Point

Color transfer, stamped, stitched, machine quilted; hand-dyed and commercial fabric, found objects; 45 by 36 in. Photo: Roger Schreiber

"Except for the point, the still point, there would be no dance, and there is only the dance."
— T. S. Eliot, *Four Quartets*

B

MARNA GOLDSTEIN BRAUNER
UNITED STATES

Deep Worrying

Photo screen printed, resist dyed, machine embroidered; antique linen, beads; 22 by 21 in. Photo: Richard Gehrke

Textiles have long been used as conveyors of information. I use text and image to make cloth objects that convey narrative experiences while alluding to both ritual and practical uses.

C

MARY LOU PEPE
UNITED STATES

Parental Poncho

Screen printed, hand and machine appliqued, pieced, quilted; hand-dyed cotton, Procion dye; 78 by 60 in. Photo: Peter F. Pepe

Wearables

Lutgardis Van der Linden
BELGIUM

Jacket
Acid-dyed, airbrushed; alpaca wool

A

ALYSON ESHELMAN
UNITED STATES

My Spring Kimono
Machine pieced and quilted; cotton Photo: Craig Kleine

B

REBEKAH YOUNGER
UNITED STATES

Ribbon Vest and Scarf
Machine knitting, painting, dyeing; rayon Photo: Martin Sobey

C

JOAN MORRIS
UNITED STATES

Tidal Pool Scarf
Arashi shibori; silk, wool, dye

D

HEIDI WOLFE
UNITED STATES

Reflecting Skin
Double weave, braided fringe; wool, cotton, antique metal thread Photo: Cathy Carver

A

B

C

D

E

JORIE JOHNSON
JAPAN

***Opulent Camouflage:
Spring Fever Set***

Felting, shibori, stitching; acid-dyed wool, printed silk organza, chenille ribbon Photo: Tsuka-hara/Standard Studio

I like children's chalk street drawings. This hand-felted fabric shows the merit of color-blending of fibers and the naive character-istics of individual yarns, as if they were lines lackadaisically drawn in chalk.

F

DEBORAH HIRD
UNITED STATES

Untitled

Handwoven, painted, stencilled, stamped; rayon, fabric paint Photo: John Cooper

E

F

D

A

JOYCE KLIMAN
UNITED STATES

Egyptian Symbols

Patchwork, machine embroidery, stencilling; cotton, velvet

B

LORRAINE JACKSON AND PAUL FRIEDMAN
UNITED STATES

Double Dip

Piecing and Seminole patchwork, beading; silk, rayon, cotton
Photo: Bill Murphy

C

KAY DISBROW
UNITED STATES

Raku

Dextrin resist, painting; silk velvet Photo: Peter Kricker (Emily Barzin, model)

D

LAURA HUHN
UNITED STATES

Dunegrass Jacket and Panel Tunic

Hand painting, block printing; silk crepe de chine Photo: Tim Eubanks

I work on a five-yard painting rack, with space heaters positioned under the hanging silk. This allows me to apply custom-blended dyes alternately on wet, dry, or semi-moist silk, depending on the effect I want.

E

KERR GRABOWSKI
UNITED STATES

Thunder Mountain Swamp

Screen print, monoprint, direct painting; silk crepe, fiber reactive dye Photo: Sean Hennessy

I attempt to make pieces strong enough to stand on their own but subtle enough to enhance, not overpower, the wearer.

E

A

Carol L. Perrenoud
UNITED STATES

Chauntecler of Cockaigne

Loom weaving; antique glass seed beads

I took photos of my favorite Aracauna rooster for color. My best possibilities for ochre, golden brown, and burnt red were in my stash of baby beads, size 20 and 22. I agonized about looming the piece, which is not my favorite technique, but decided finally that I would get the best result that way.

B

Diane B. Kribs-Mays
UNITED STATES

Wings

Peyote stitch, bead netting; glass beads, nylon thread Photo: Clix Photographs

C

Don Pierce
UNITED STATES

Surreal Butterfly

Loom weaving; antique seed and nailhead beads (center bead handmade by Tom Boylam)
Photo: Martin Kilmer

B

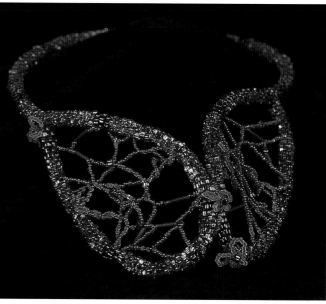

A

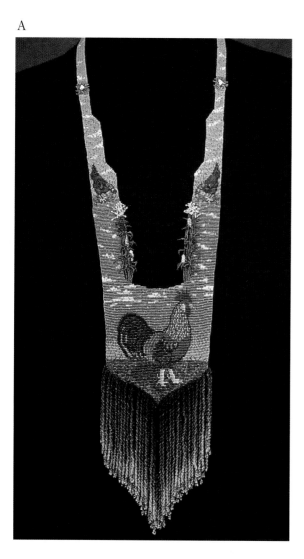

C

D

ANN BROOKS
UNITED STATES

Cord Necklace
Spool knitting; silver, gold
Photo: Hap Sakwa

*I am drawn to creating sculptural
forms. Knit or lace wire is the
perfect medium—as a fiber, it's
flexible; as metal, it holds its
shape. The jewelry looks fragile,
yet it's tough.*

E

BONNIE A. BERKOWITZ
UNITED STATES

Wristwords: Book Bracelet
Fusing, stitching, embroidery;
cotton, glass beads, waxed linen
Photo: Peter Fornabai

*The outside is weighted and cool
to the touch, while the inside—
the shadow side of
the piece's story—is warm,
embroidered writing.*

F

JUDITH R. SHAMP
UNITED STATES

Magicicada
Cutting, fusing; synthetic fabric,
netting, ultrasuede, vintage buttons Photo: Mike McCormick

*Using a variety of manipulation
techniques, including working
with a hot knife and
pleater/smocker, I've made a wide
range of different-sized "bugs."*

G

ARLENE GITOMER
UNITED STATES

Hooked
Sewing, painting; hand-pulled
paper, linen, cotton, paint, beads

*My textile jewelry is influenced by
the emotional impact of the free
and easy lines of Oriental callig-
raphy and patterns.*

D

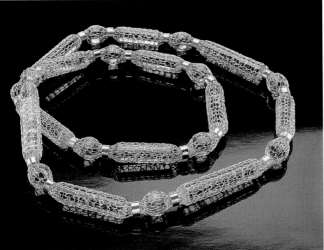

E

F

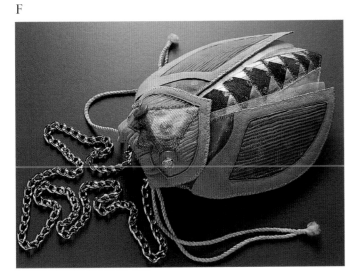

G

A

PIA FILLIGER-NOLTE
GERMANY

Dress
Ondulée weaving; cashmere/silk
Photo: Georg Jahnke

B

CAROL MCKIE MANNING
UNITED STATES

Bahia de La Paz
Hand dyeing, painting, stamping, embroidery, beading; silk chiffon, Thai silk, ultrasuede, beads Photo: Tom Henderson (Willow Buckley, model)

The amazing colors of the Bay of La Paz and the Sea of Cortez— teal, turquoise, aquamarine, royal blue—were the inspiration for this piece.

C

ELVIRA VIRANYI-SCHUBERT
GERMANY

Rainbow Dress
Sewing, painting; silk velvet
Photo: Hajott

Shape, design, and color have to harmonize for an "aura" like a rainbow.

D

JOAN MCGEE
UNITED STATES

Antiquity
Pole wrapped, pleated, overdyed, fused; linen Photo: John Cooper

E

TERI JO AND CARTER SMITH
UNITED STATES

Bad Hairday Bag and *Cut Satin Dress*
Discharge shibori, cut satin (dress by Carter); Japanese silk (bag by Teri Jo) Photo: Carolyn Ross

F

ERZSEBET KATONA SZABO
HUNGARY

Pompous Dress
Applique, embroidery; silk

This dress was inspired by the splendor of ancient tinted pottery.

A

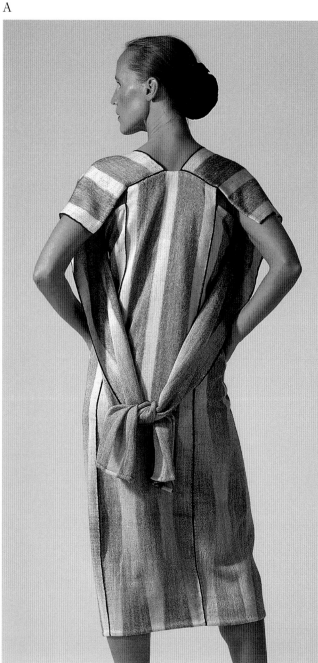

B

C

D

E

F

A

B

A

FAYE ANDERSON
UNITED STATES

Tromsø—Midnight Sun *(and detail)*
Strip pieced, layered, sewn, embellished; handwoven wool (by Yvonne Stahl), metallic organza, beads
Photo: Joe Coca

B

CARYNE FINLAY
UNITED STATES

Mrs. Arakawa's Longevity Coat
Machine construction, top stitching, beading; Japanese kimono silk, glass seed beads, charms Photo: Debora Cartwright, The Darkroom

In Mrs. Arakawa's life so far, major events seem to occur every 18 years, so I incorporated beads and buttons in numbers that add up or multiply to 18. When the coat is turned inside-out to display its reverse side, for example, there are 18 buttons up the back.

C

D

C

PEGGOTTY CHRISTENSEN
UNITED STATES

Mimbres Jacket

Devoré, hand painting;
rayon/silk velvet Photo: Bruce
Talbot

*The devoré technique has
allowed me to create fabric
with another dimension, and
to design specifically for each
garment. I begin with white
rayon and silk velvet or satin
and paint the burnout solution
on the fabric with brushes,
designing to relate to the shape
of the garment. After processing the fabric, I paint it with
dyes and finally sew the piece.*

D

CYNTHIA WAYNE GAFFIELD
UNITED STATES

Tomato Coat

Hand painting and stamping,
machine stitching and quilting;
Tussah silk, Procion dyes
Photo: Craig Gaffield

E

JOANNA CHRYSOHOIDIS
UNITED STATES

Are We There Yet?

Handwoven, warp and surface
painting; Procion dyes, cotton,
fiber paint Photo: Jim Osen

E

A

ANN SHEIKH
UNITED STATES

Deco Bride
Quilting, dye painting; silk Photo:
Judy Hailey

*This is a wedding ensemble
inspired by a 1920s bride.*

B

PATTY GALLAGHER
UNITED STATES

The Empress
Sewing, construction; silk flowers
Photo: Tom Little

A

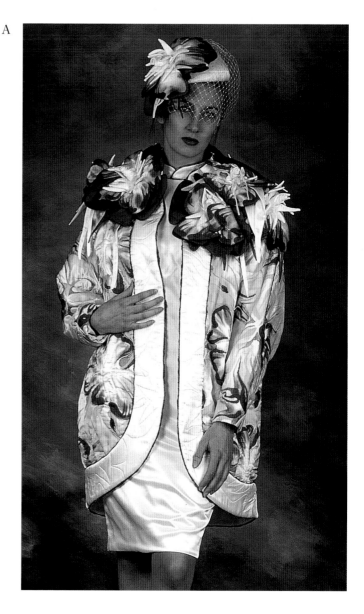

B

C

NIKKI WILLIS
ENGLAND

Spike Dress
Shibori, machine stitching, hand
and machine embroidery; silk,
dyes, paints

*I have always loved the bizarre
and unusual, and this has been
the biggest motivation for me to
produce eyecatching, if somewhat macabre, clothing and
accessories.*

D

JULIA SOUBBOTINA
GERMANY

Fire
Sewing, painting; organza, wire

Although the costume is an objet
d'art *in the first place, the fire
lights only when ignited by the
movement of a body. The torso
of the dress is elliptical and con-
sists of a number of small sections. Whenever the body moves,
these sections start to shiver.*

E

PETER CIESLA
UNITED STATES

Anemone
Piecing, beading; wool, cotton,
silk, wood and glass beads

F

SHA SHA HIGBY
UNITED STATES

Tea on a Twig
Construction; paper, silk, wood,
patinas

C

D

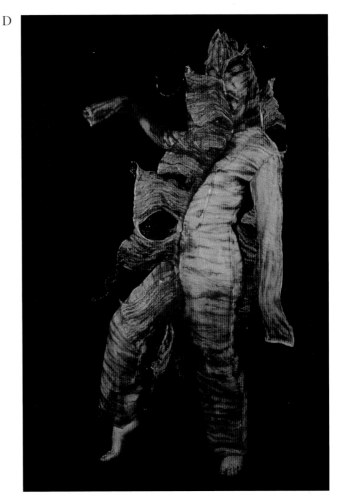

E

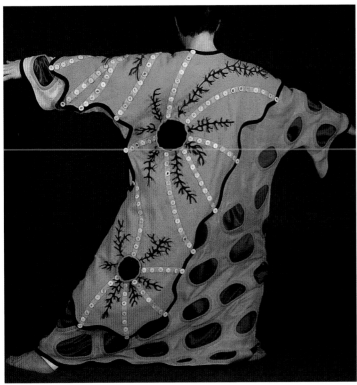

F

A

B

C

D

E

A

RISA BENSON
UNITED STATES

Large Clutch Purse
Hook woven, drop stitch; mixed
rayon yarns, sterling silver Photo:
George Erml

B

YVONNE WAKABAYASHI
CANADA

Arashi Shibori Vest
Pleating, screen printing, bond-
ing, machine embroidery; silk
Photo: Barbara Cohen

*My interest is in the layering of
surface design techniques—both
Japanese and Western ideas.*

C

CINDY WALSH
UNITED STATES

Barn Coat and Beret
Applique; binding, trims, wind-
proof polar fleece Photo: Bob
Barrett

D

LAURA HUHN
UNITED STATES

Untitled Tie Collection
Hand painting, block printing;
silk crepe de chine Photo: George
Post

E

LESLEY HANSARD AND
REBECCA WELSH
UNITED STATES

Bulb Hat
Hand felting; merino wool

*Hansard Welsh Design hats are
meant to be fun, warm, and pri-
marily a fashion statement. Our
inspiration is endless; crazy
dreams, old movies, and the need
to break the day-to-day monot-
ony of drab and boring headwear.*

F

SARAH F. SAULSON
UNITED STATES

Windowpane Scarf
Multi-structure weave, painted
warp, hand-plied rope fringe
Photo: David Coulter

G

ADRIENNE SLOANE
UNITED STATES

Siberian Rose
Machine knitting, hand finishing;
rayon chenille, cotton

*I am most drawn to the sculp-
tural aspects of knit. I love
exploring the outer limits of
design and find it wonderful that
this is all done with a single
strand of yarn.*

F

G

A

Erica Spitzer Rasmussen
UNITED STATES

Totemic Coat

Assembling, sewing; paper, watermelon seeds, shower curtain; 69 by 70 by 3 in. Photo: Dan Kahler

Like the Asante hunting jackets of Ghana, this garment was created to protect me from evil and injury.

B

Darlene H. Skog
UNITED STATES

Indigo Jacket

Machine piecing, pleating, hand sewing, sashika; Japanese antique fabrics, Thai handwoven cotton, commercial cotton, Vogue Designer pattern (Issey Miyaki) Photo: Bill Bachhuber

A

B

C

Linda O'Leary-Allen
UNITED STATES

A Coat of Inspiration

Silkscreen, chemical resist; Indian silk, silk satin Photo: Catherine C. Walker

C

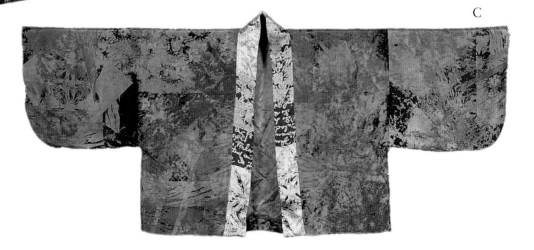

D

JEAN NAPIER
SOUTH AFRICA

Ecclesiastical Jacket
Hand knitting; silk, wool,
angora, mohair, alpaca Photo:
Mark Napier

E

GALE NEHRIG
UNITED STATES

Fifth Avenue
Multi-harness weaving, sum-
mer/winter technique; cotton,
wool Photo: Joe Comick

F

ROBIN L. BERGMAN
UNITED STATES

Woodblock Tunic and Scarf
Loom knitting; rayon chenille,
rayon/silk noil
Photo: Gordon S. Bernstein

D

E

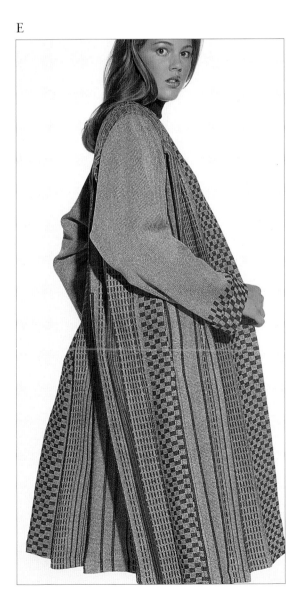

F

A

FERN WAYNE
UNITED STATES

Chenille Scarves
Machine knitting; wool, rayon
Photo: G. Thomas Murray

B

WAYNE WICHERN
UNITED STATES

Bad Apple
Hand blocking and beading;
velour felt, glass beads (beaded
worm by David Chatt) Photo:
Larry Stessin

C

ANN DE VUONO
UNITED STATES

Spectator with Poppy
Weaving, stitching; silk
charmeuse Photo: Michael
Doucett
*This piece was inspired by the
spectator pumps to which I
aspired when I was wearing saddle shoes in my Catholic school
days. The saddle shoes were sup-
posed to provoke linear perfec-
tion in all my thoughts, but a
poppy seed blew in.*

A

B

C

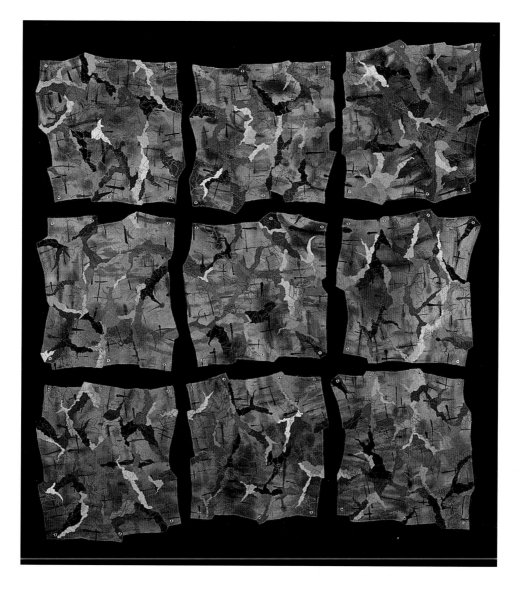

STEPHANIE RANDALL COOPER
UNITED STATES

Nine Patch: Fortitude

Construction, machine quilting; dyed hemp/silk, cotton, rayon;
78 by 78 in. Photo: Mark Frey

*We sometimes need the strength of moral and spiritual conviction just to
get through the day. This piece is part of the "Survival Skills" series*

A

Aune Taamal
ESTONIA

The Divine Love
Weaving, warp painting and
printing; linen, cotton, wool;
119 by 47¼ in.

B

K. Sarah Kaufmann
UNITED STATES

Weird Mist
Weaving, warp painting; cotton;
36 by 30 in. Photo: Mimi
Yamasaki

A

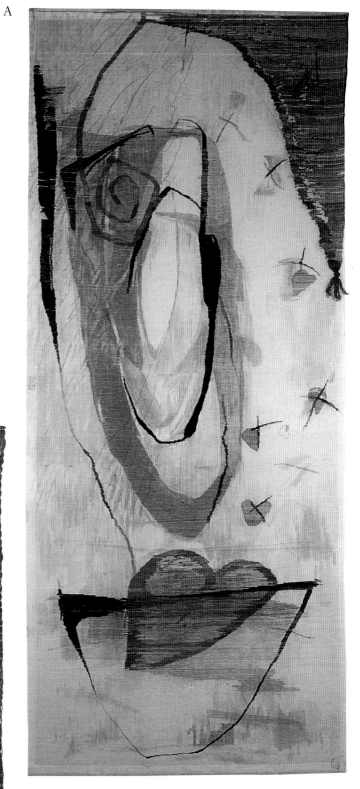

B

C

C

ROSLYN LOGSDON
UNITED STATES

Vins des Rues II
Hooking; wool; 21 by 19 in.
Photo: Linda Zandler

*It was a celebration of the
Beaujolais nouveau. Three
friends met for drinks and
conversation. One fellow came
for the food.*

D

AIJA BAUMANE
LATVIA

Time (and detail)
Weaving; wool, linen,
synthetics; 61 by 57 in.

D

A

NANCY BELFER
UNITED STATES

Coded Wall
Collage; paper, fabric, paint; 15
by 30 in.

B

LESLIE GABRIËLSE
THE NETHERLANDS

Tomatoes on a Vine
Applique, painting; fabric, acrylic
paint; 57 by 75 in.

A

B

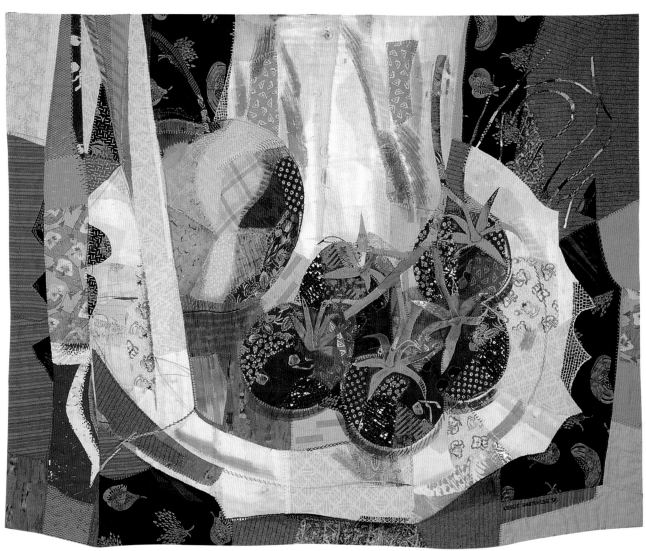

C

C

DAVID B. BRACKETT
UNITED STATES

Water Under the Bridge
Weaving; warp painting, polychromatic screen printing, photo screen printing, machine stitching; cotton, fiber reactive dyes, textile pigments; 71 by 55 in.

Our lives are filled with chance occurrences. I am intrigued by the way that seemingly random processes produce order and pattern, and by the fact that the forces that shape rivers, produce stripes on a tiger, and control the formation of snowflakes are the same ones that control political, economic, and social systems.

D

D

REBECCA J. VORIS
UNITED STATES

Next Door (and detail)
Brocade weave, airbrushed; cotton, dyes; 66 by 22⅛ in.
Photo: David Wharton

Primitive art has influenced both the subjects and compositions of my recent work. The figures are deeply personal but also suggest fantasy. I proceed intuitively, making a mark with a piece of yarn and following the image wherever it takes me. This is from my "High Rise" series.

A

ANNE HUEBEL
GERMANY

Simplicity of Lines
Leno weave; cotton/silk

B

CAMERON TAYLOR-
BROWN
UNITED STATES

Hopscotch
Weaving, stitchery; linen, cotton,
rayon, mesh, wood, paint; 58 by
48 in. Photo: "Q"

*My artwork reflects a constant
desire to shape order out of
chaos—to create something
complex and satisfying where
nothing existed before.*

A

B

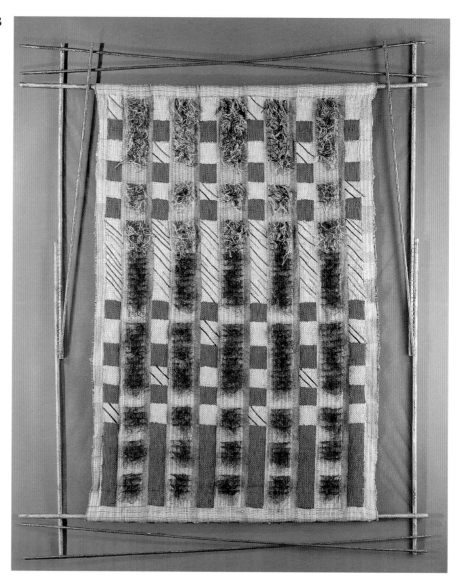

C

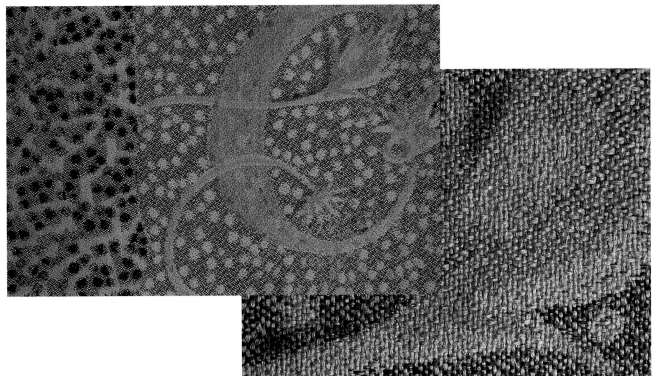

D

C
FUYUKO MATSUBARA
UNITED STATES

The Dew I *(and detail)*
Weaving, warp and weft painting;
hand-plied yarn of linen, cotton,
ramie, silk, rayon; 18 by 29 in.

*I wanted to depict two spaces
existing simultaneously. They are
like underground and
overground. They seem quite
different and separate; however,
they do not exist without each
other.*

D
GUGGER PETTER
UNITED STATES

Waiting #2
Weaving; newspaper on hemp;
74 by 68 in.

A

A

IRINA KOLESNIKOVA
RUSSIA

On the move
Hand weaving; linen, silk;
6 by 10 in.

*There are some folk somewhere
that are strange and a bit funny.
They are busy with their travels,
families, political events, and
leavetakings. They wear funny
shoes with heels and know
nothing about us.*

B

OLGA L. ROTHSCHILD
UNITED STATES

Mr. Blue
Hand hooking; wool, linen
(recycled clothing); 31 by 39 in.
Photo: David Bitters

*This was inspired by a drawing
by my grandson.*

C

LAURA WILLITS
UNITED STATES

The Visitor
Weaving; glass seed beads;
13½ by 9½ in.

*Comet Hale-Bopp was so
beautiful! I'm glad I was here to
witness its visit.*

D

JANE A. EVANS
CANADA

Cattail Corner
Weaving, warp painting,
embroidery; cotton, rayon,
polyester, silk, fabric paint; 7¾
by 10⅛ in. Photo: AK Photo

*The small wetland is depicted in
painted warps, an assortment of
textural woven threads, and
embroidery done in both
weaving and sewing threads.*

E

LINDA RAE COUGHLIN
UNITED STATES

The Blues
Hooking; wool, linen;
35 by 48 in.

B

C

D

E

A

Patty Yoder
UNITED STATES

V is for Victor—A Natural Vegetarian
Hooking; wool; 42 by 51 in.
Photo: Bill Bishop

B

Patricia Malarcher
UNITED STATES

Doors and Windows
(and detail)
Machine and hand sewing,
piecing, sponge printing; mylar,
fabric, found materials; 60 by 60
in. Photo: D. James Dee

*The square collages are like
fragments of my life.*

C

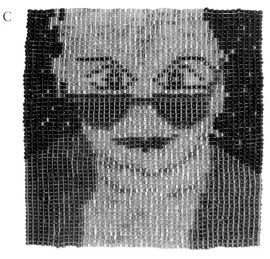

C

AASE VASLOW
UNITED STATES

M One
Bead loom weaving; beads, linen;
4 by 4 in. Photo: Fred Vaslow

*Each of the pieces in this series is
a lighthearted portrait of a close
friend whose name begins with
an "M."*

D

KATHY DAVIE
UNITED STATES

Mi Casita (and detail)
Hand and machine applique,
machine piecing and quilting,
embroidery; lace, upholstery
fabric, yarn, silk ribbon, hand-
dyed and commercial cotton,
textile inks; 26 by 43 in. Photo:
John Bonath

D

A

DIANNE SHULLENBERGER
UNITED STATES

Fall Trees

Layered collage; silk, cotton, organza; 18 by 15 in. Photo: Lori Landau

B

LAURA BREITMAN
UNITED STATES

Breeze in Tall Grass

Collage, frottage; hand-printed and commercial fabric, polymer varnish; 18 by 24 in.

I have two goals in mind when I work on my collages. One is to fool the eye and the other is to choose an image that presents me with a challenge.

C

ROBERT FORMAN
UNITED STATES

Nierica (and detail)

Yarn painting; cotton, silk, linen, rayon thread, glue; 60 in. diameter. Photo: Jeff Goldman

The circular format is the shape of traditional Huichol prayer offerings. The sun is surrounded by a landscape based on the community of Santa Caterina, and the border is composed of images of Huichol people I've met, interwoven with symbols and images of their art. The word nierica is derived from a Huichol word signifying a visionary ability facilitated by a small round mirror.

A

B

C

A

MARINA NETCHEPORUK
RUSSIA

My Italy (Venice I) *(and detail)*
Hand weaving; linen, silk, metal, photographs; 19¾ by 15¾ in.

The past and the present, the imagination and reality, the dreams and visions are the threads of my artistic credo.

B

MARIE-NOELLE FONTAN
FRANCE

Lunaria *(and detail)*
Weaving; cotton, lunaria seeds; 11½ by 9 in. Photo: Guillermo Escalon

I don't know if plant life has any kind of language. By weaving with two natural components, I am trying to create a dialogue between them.

A

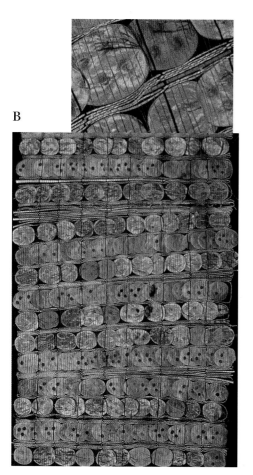

B

C

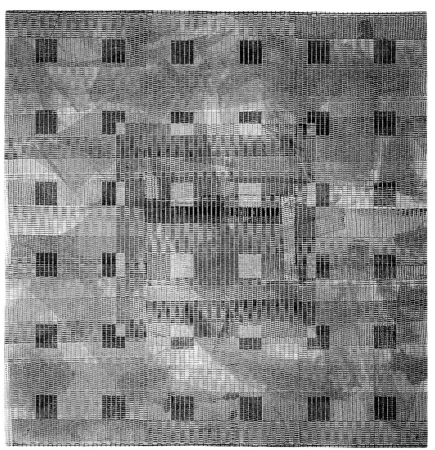

D

C

Pauline Verbeek-
Cowart
United States

Cycles #1

Weaving, screen printing; cotton
and polypropylene yarn, paper,
textile pigments; 55 by 55 in.

*The "Cycles" series constitutes an
exploration of recurring events.
Blocks of threads in the warp
create a predictable repeat
pattern across the surface. Most
thread groupings are identical but
appear to be different due to the
interaction of warp and weft.
This emulates the concept of
cycles in nature, as nature repeats
itself but never in quite the same
way, due to ever-changing
circumstances.*

D

Victoria Bere
England

Urban Heroes

Weaving, warp printing; cotton,
polyester, wool; 15 by 12 in.
Photo: Howard Fox

*This piece was based on 1930s
film noir—past memories,
treasured and precious, but
partly faded. Heroes provided a
form of escapism from reality.*

E

Janice Lessman-Moss
United States

I Dreamed I Was Flying

Weaving, warp painting; linen,
cotton, metal wire; 65 by 63 in.

E

A

ANNE MARIE KENNY
UNITED STATES

Woven Needle Holder II
Industrial Quilt
Weaving, hand stitching; wire-
cloth, sewing machine needles; 31
by 32 in. Photo: Jack Bingham

B

PAMELA E. BECKER
UNITED STATES

Falling Water
Piecing, applique, painting,
machine and hand stitching;
cotton/polyester duck, organza,
ribbon, acrylic paint;
56 by 57 x 6 in.

C

MAKIKO WAKISAKA
JAPAN

Cloudy Sunrise
Machine and hand stitching,
dyeing; water soluble cloth, nylon
thread; 49 by 49 in. Photo:
Katsuro Takahashi

I create leaf vein imagery because
I think it is a symbol of the life
force. It looks delicate, but
actually has strong power inside.

D

BARBARA WALKER
CANADA

Street Dance
Weaving, supplementary warp
pick-up; mercerized cotton;
22 by 29 in.

E

GLORIA E. CROUSE
UNITED STATES

Fusion
Tufting, sculpting; wool,
metal; 96 by 108 in.

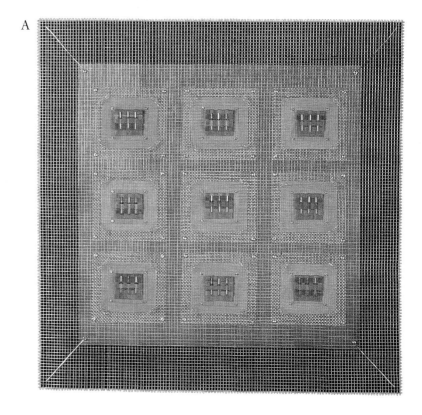

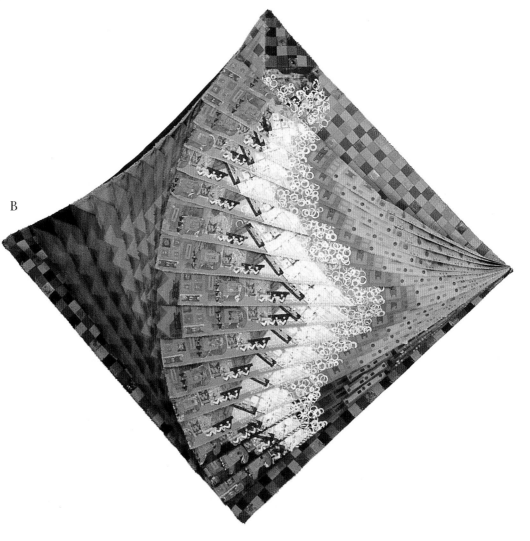

A

B

C

A

PEG IRISH
UNITED STATES

The Ann and Peg Show
Hooked rug, appliqued, collaged,
photo transfer; wool and cotton,
found objects; 20 by 22 in.

*The work commemorates my
long friendship with fellow rug
hooker, Ann Winterling. Even
though we no longer live in the
same state, we look for
opportunities to reunite,
including attending an occasional
workshop together. This piece
was inspired by a photo taken at
one such workshop.*

B

ELIZABETH G. KUHN
UNITED STATES

Dilemma
Quadruple weave pick-up,
painted warps and wefts; cotton;
47½ by 40 in. Photo: Mike
Sperko

*We are caught between the desire
to keep everything we earn and
the necessity of paying taxes for
the improvement of the society as
a whole.*

D

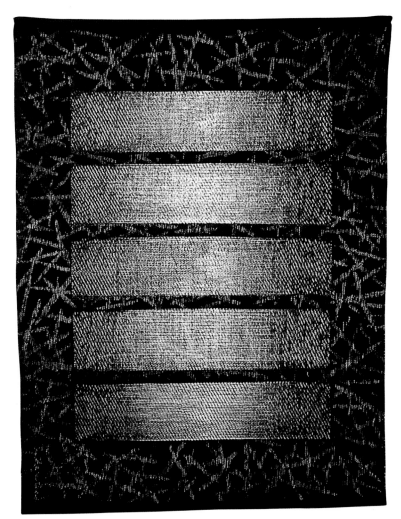

C

KYOUNG AE CHO
UNITED STATES

Quilt?! – III
Sewn, sliced and drilled wood;
waxed linen, wood, construction
board; 54 by 54 in.

*Time and nurturing are carried
through the rings of wisdom.
These patterns allow the viewer
to visualize the existence and
environmental history of this tree
and how it has sheltered and
nurtured the earth.*

D

KYUNG-NAM CHOI
UNITED STATES

Reminiscence – V
Weaving, supplementary weft
brocade, discharge dyeing;
cotton; 45 by 36 in. Photo:
Barbara Molloy

E

**MARTHA DONOVAN
OPDAHL**
UNITED STATES

Sua
Tufting, dyeing; wool;
53½ by 79 in.

E

A

NANCY MIDDLEBROOK
UNITED STATES

Untitled

Doubleweave, ikat; cotton; 15 by
23 in. Photo: Paul G. Joslin

B

DAVID WEIDIG
UNITED STATES

Daybreak at the City Diner
(and detail)

Interlacing, stitching, stenciling,
collage; paper, acrylic paint,
cotton; 102 by 59 in.

A

B

C

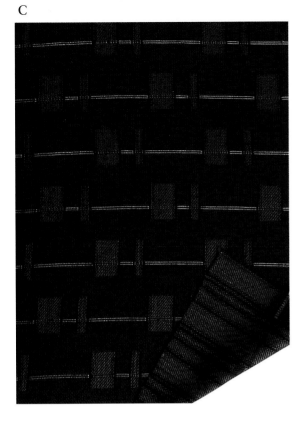

C

GILLIAN GURNEY
ENGLAND

Abstract 2
Backed weave (variation) with
extra warp; silk

*Reversible fabrics have endless
possibilities.*

D

KATRIN PERE
ESTONIA

Very Busy Tapestry (and detail)
Mixed techniques; silk, cotton,
synthetics; 63 by 63 in.

*My father's jacket was the
starting point for this piece. A
business suit has served Its
owner, it has served its time, and
it is now a symbol of the
beautiful life of my father.*

D

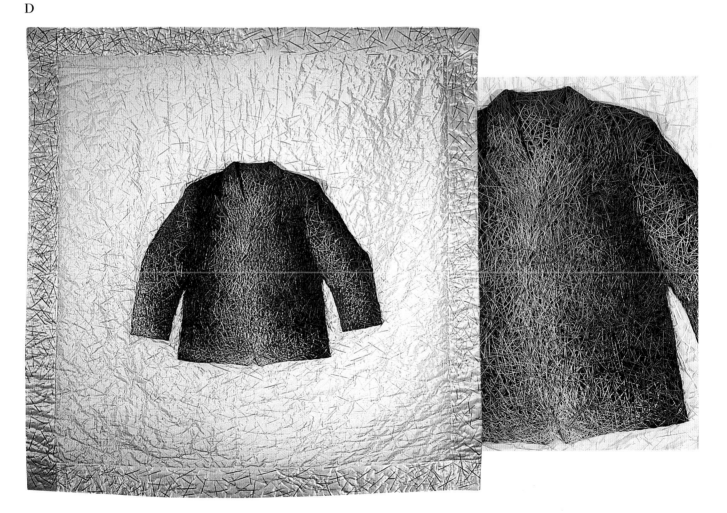

Barbara Simon
UNITED STATES

Heleconia and the Rainforest
Weaving, weft inlay; linen, silk,
rayon, abaca cloth, reeds;
26 by 32 in. Photo: Red Elf

*Working within the tradition of
textiles, I use fiber as a means of
expressing my concerns for the
rainforests and the alarming rate
of their destruction. The inclusion
of text is to help convey the
urgency of the message.*

B

Marisa Bronzini
ITALY

Filo 66
Weaving; silk, cotton, linen;
50 by 60 in.

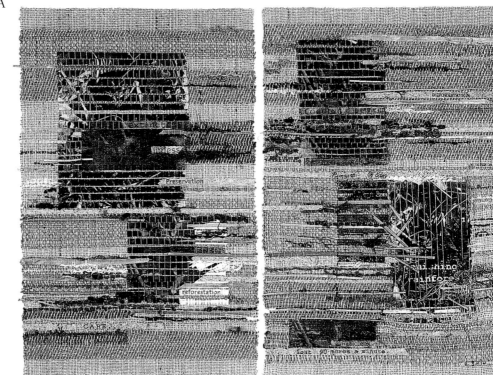

C

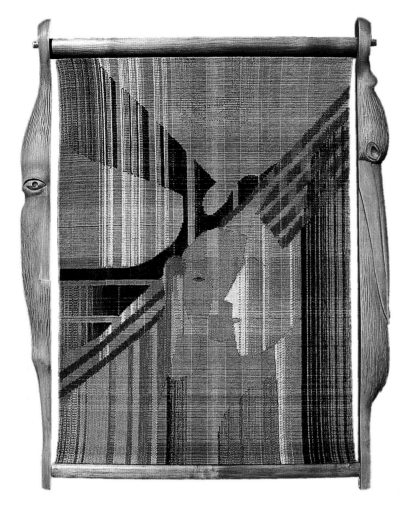

C

PETER HORSFALL
ENGLAND

Thoughts
Moorman technique; cotton,
wool, silk; 38 by 28 in.

D

KATHLEEN M. ROIG
UNITED STATES

Protection
Weaving, warp and weft
painting, sewing; cotton,
handmade paper, fabric paint,
found objects; 26 by 26 in.

*I used materials that I have made
(the paper, the fabric) along with
elements collected that are
important to me (the shells from
my son during a vacation to the
beach).*

D

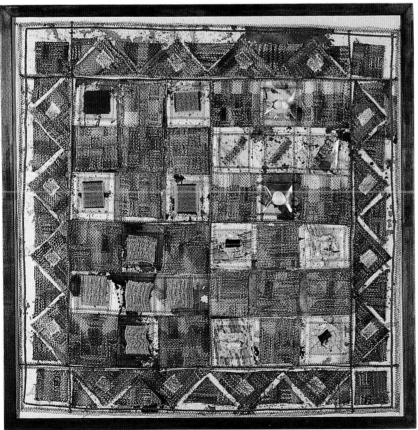

A

LOUISE LEMIEUX BERUBE
CANADA

Joe
Jacquard weaving; cotton, linen;
64 by 43 in.

B

KONYA KINGA
HUNGARY

Fingerprint
Jacquard weaving; cotton;
59 by 49 in.

*It is a print of my left thumb
(never used by the police).*

C

LOUISE LEMIEUX BERUBE
CANADA

La La La Human Steps
Jacquard weaving; cotton, linen;
60 by 43 in.

D

KAROLY ZÖLD GYÖNGYI
ROMANIA

Genesis in Black
Machine knitting; acrylic yarn;
88½ by 38½ in.

E

CAROL D. WESTFALL
UNITED STATES

The Canadians
Jacquard weaving; cotton; 30 by
24 in. Photo: D. James Dee

*I altered a newspaper image on
the computer. Canadians can now
go topless on their beaches, and
this celebrates that freedom.*

A

B

C

D

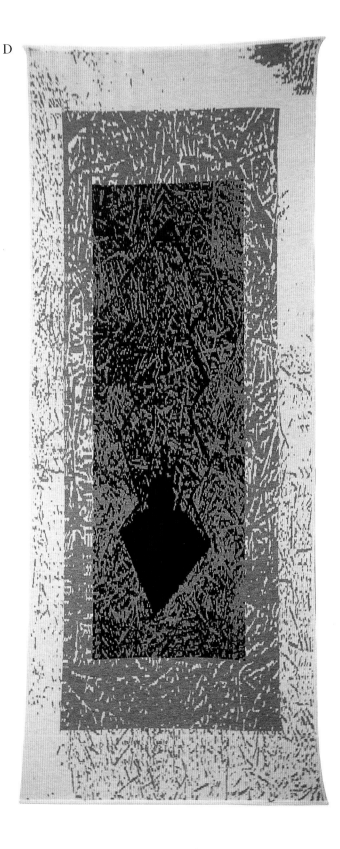

E

A

SHARON McCARTNEY
UNITED STATES

Quiet Bursts of Enthusiasm
Collage, painting, printing,
machine and hand sewing;
handmade and commercial paper,
netting, fabric; 31 by 17 in.
Photo: Apex Design

*My strong connection to nature
has been a great source of
inspiration, creating an arena for
play, escape, spirituality, and the
continuous study of colors,
shapes, textures, and repetitive
patterns.*

B

CATHARINE ELLIS
MUERDTER
UNITED STATES

Vision (and detail)
Weaving, resist-dyed; cotton,
indigo; 89 by 46 in.
Photo: Tim Barnwell

*The technique of woven shibori
resist combines, in the truest
sense, the loom-woven patterned
cloth with the surface design
process of applying dye.*

B

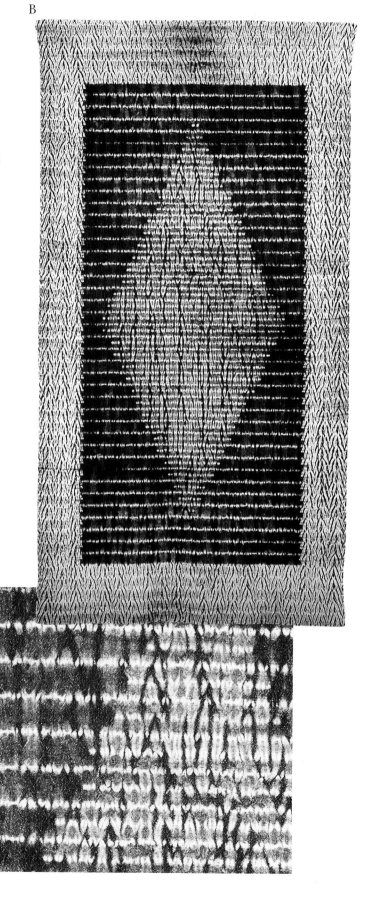

A

C

C

CATHERINE DWORE
UNITED STATES

Crop Succession
Collage; fabric, metallic foil;
25 by 33½ in.
Photo: Charley Freiberg

*In Florida, the disappearance of
farmland is followed, almost
overnight, by rampant urban
growth.*

D

LINDA SENECHAL
UNITED STATES

Sea of Reflection
Weaving, warp painting,
embroidery; cotton, linen, rayon;
31 by 70 in. Photo: David Caras

D

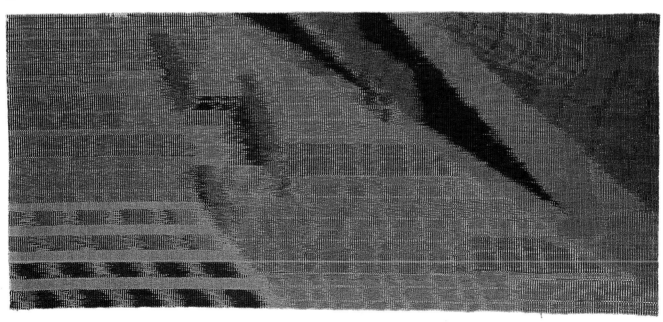

A

ERICA LICEA-KANE
UNITED STATES

Bullseye

Weaving, layering; wool, lace,
rice paper, acrylic medium;
54 by 58 in. Photo: David Caras

B

ARLYN ENDE
UNITED STATES

Spirit Wing

Collage; dyed fabric, handmade
paper, acrylic paint; 22 by 18 in.
Photo: Jim Ann Howard

C

EMILY K. ROBERTSON
UNITED STATES

Chelsea Garden

Hand dyeing and hooking; wool;
59 by 46 in.

A

C

B

TAPESTRY

BETTY VERA
UNITED STATES

Silently I Wait
Tapestry, painted and supplementary warp, mixed weaves; cotton; 50 by 40 in.
Photo: Adam Reich

This is the first of several tapestries I have designed based on my feelings about my mother's death. Its title is taken from the words to the hymn "Open My Eyes," which she had requested for her memorial service. The text, which is a prayer for divine release, made me think of a bird or other winged creature, spreading its wings upward, toward freedom.

A

SARAH SWETT
UNITED STATES

Luncheon Under the Elms
Tapestry; hand spun wool and
mohair, natural dyes; 46 by 60 in.
Photo: Mark La Moreaux

*Kids—you love them to death, but
they certainly can (and will) inter-
rupt an interesting conversation.*

B

BEATA HAUSER
HUNGARY

Group Picture
Gobelin tapestry; wool; 43 by
80½ in. Collection of Hungarian
Nationale Bank, Budapest

C

MARIA SCHNEIDER-SENJUK
UKRAINE

Apple Orchard
Tapestry; wool warp, cotton weft;
94½ by 138 in.

D

EMMA JO WEBSTER
SCOTLAND

Piensando de mis amigos
Tapestry; wool, cotton, lurex; 36
by 84 in.

*The people shown are a cross sec-
tion of friends and family, varying
from people I hardly know to very
good, lifelong friends.*

A

B

C

D

A

RUTH MANNING
UNITED STATES

Rowena
Tapestry; wool, cotton; 20 by
20 in. Photo: Richard Margolis

B

YURI SCHNEIDER
UKRAINE

On the River Bank
Tapestry; wool warp, cotton
weft; 51½ by 45 in.

C

FELIKSAS JAKUBAUSKAS
LITHUANIA

Kitty, Kitty, My Little Cat
Gobelin tapestry; wool, silk,
synthetics; 51 by 73 in. Photo:
Antanas Luksenas

D

D

CANADA

Tsk, Tsk
Tapestry; linen warp, wool weft;
34 by 48 in.

*"Do unto others as you would
have them do unto you."*

E

ANDREW SCHNEIDER
KHERSON, UKRAINE

In Front of the Lilac Mirror
Tapestry; wool, cotton; 47 by 63 in.

E

A

MARTA ROGOYSKA
UNITED STATES

Courtyard 7
High warp Gobelin tapestry; cotton warp, wool weft; 37 by 37 in. Photo: Ricardo Dante

B

HELGA BERRY
UNITED STATES

Beyond the Blue
Tapestry; silk, synthetics, wool; 39 by 39 in. Photo: Chris Arend Photography

I love the process of tapestry-making. The solid construction of an image from a heap of yarn is a most rewarding experience.

C

AUDREY MOORE
UNITED STATES

Dependence
Tapestry; wool warp, hand-dyed wool weft; 37 by 47 in. Photo: Dennis Purdy

D

CARE STANDLEY
UNITED STATES

Chained Up, Tied Down
Tapestry; wool, cotton; 18 by 24 in. Photo: Kim Harrington

E

CHARLOTTE ZIEBARTH
UNITED STATES

Night on Bald Mountain
Slit tapestry, embroidery; wool warp, wool, silk, rayon, cotton weft; 60 by 60 in.

The subtitle of this work is ...and Other Fears of the Night. I have recurring dreams of ladders that have rungs missing but the need to climb them anyway. In my awake state, I have a strong fear of heights.

A

B

C

D

E

A

JUDY SCHUSTER
UNITED STATES

*It Depends on Your Point of
View III* (two views)
Tapestry, folding; linen warp,
wool weft, metal rods; 36 by 25
in. Photo: Andrew Neuhardt

*The subject of my work is
duality—the mysteries and
ambiguities, and conflict and
complements arising from
opposites within one person or
between people.*

B

BARBARA HELLER
CANADA

Resonance
Tapestry; linen warp, hand-dyed
linen weft; 54 by 41 in.

*The boundaries of time, space,
and spirit can be crossed, but at
what price? A young Buddhist
monk hurries through an old
European archway in Peru. The
past is in ruins. He steps over the
rubble; his gaze is inward as he
leans into the future.*

C

SHELLEY SOCOLOFSKY
UNITED STATES

Crease
Gobelin tapestry; cotton warp,
wool and silk weft; 84 by 42 in.

D

SOYOO HYUNJOO PARK
UNITED STATES

Korean Dancers
Hachures tapestry; cotton warp,
cotton, wool weft; 48 by 120 in.

A

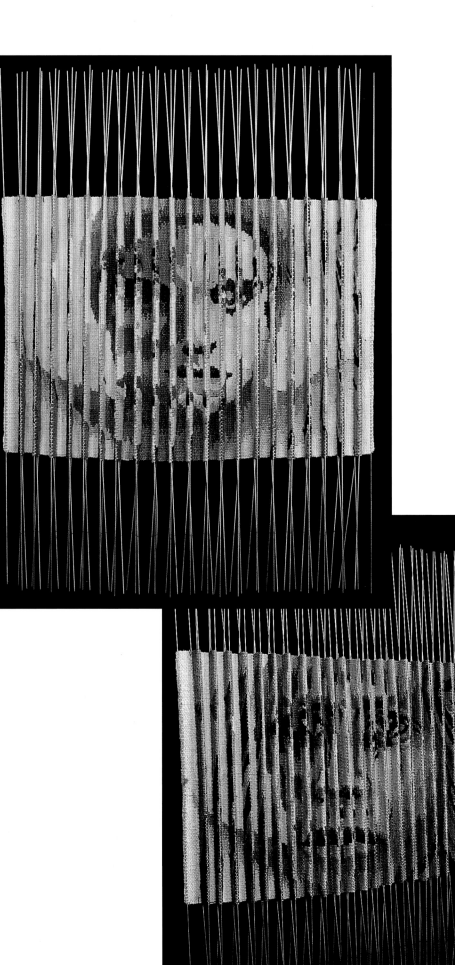

B

C

D

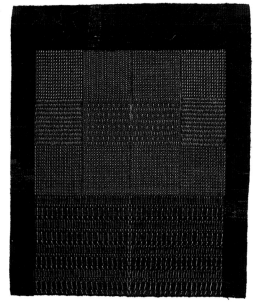

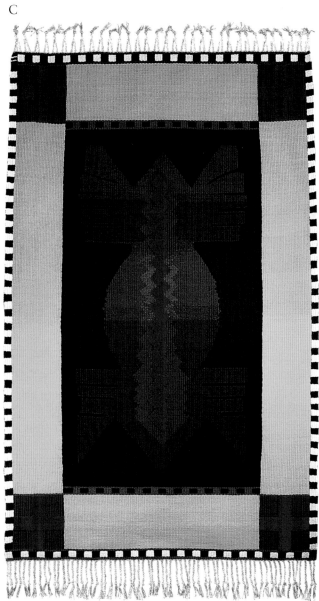

E

F

A

ANNE ADAMS
UNITED STATES

Soup

Tapestry; wool warp, handspun, hand-dyed wool weft; 32½ by 39 in. Photo: Mark La Moreaux

A beautiful spring day does not make me wish for my kitchen, but it does make me want to dance and to weave, and it lights up my entire life.

B

ANNE MCGINN
UNITED STATES

Green Silk Coat: Seaside Poems for Emily

Eccentric weft tapestry; cotton; 77 by 65 in. Photo: Michael Scarpelli

C

FRANZISKA KURTH
GERMANY

Meeting Place: Women's Bath

Gobelin/kilim tapestry; linen, wool, cotton, silk; 65 by 39 in.

I like to put situations from daily life in tapestry, using metaphors from fairy tales and situations I have experienced or seen some-where. Using a kind of comic style, I like to simplify the subjects because in tapestry techniques, they become more expressive.

I made this tapestry after spend-ing some time in a sauna for women only....

D

ANNE JACKSON
ENGLAND

Old Master

Knotted tapestry; cotton, linen, synthetic yarns; 60 by 36 in. Photo: Paul Constant

Textiles are still mostly made by women. My work comments on the place of women and textiles in the arts and in the world.

E

PETER HARRIS
CANADA

Triumph of ... Whatever

Tapestry; linen warp, wool weft; 60 by 96 in.

B

C

D

E

A

MARINA KRUCHININA
RUSSIA

Nature Piece
Tapestry; wool, linen; 33 by 27
in. Photo: Sergei Petrov

*There is deliberate, defiant sim-
plicity in nature.*

B

KAIJA RAUTIAINEN
CANADA

Autumn Metamorphosis
(and detail)
Tapestry; linen; 40 by 40 in.

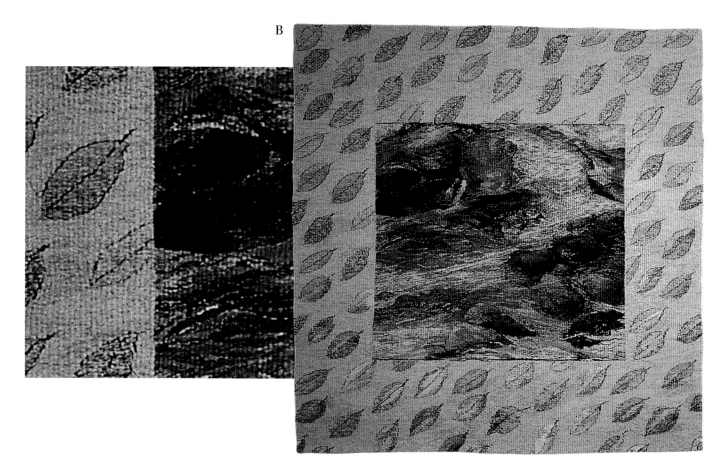

C

C

NANCY JACKSON
UNITED STATES

City/Country II
Gobelin/Aubusson tapestry; cotton warp, wool weft; 18 by 28 in.

D

DONNA MARTIN
UNITED STATES

A Letter Home
Tapestry; wool, mohair, vegetal dye; 63½ by 47 in.
Photo: Pat Pollard

E

BARBARA LEWIS
UNITED STATES

Persian II
Tapestry; cotton warp, wool weft, embroidery floss;
15 by 11½ in.
Photo: Richard McCrary

A

MARTHA MATTHEWS
UNITED STATES

*Contemplating the Coastal
Plain*

Tapestry; cotton warp, wool,
linen, cotton; 46½ by 64¼ in.

*This tapestry deals with the loss
of identity a woman experiences
when she moves because of her
husband. It challenges the assump-
tion that wide open space is free-
ing and exhilarating; actually, a
vast empty landscape can be very
confining for a city person. It is
also about new beginnings.*

B

LOIS KENNEDY
CANADA

Redberry County

Gobelin tapestry, embroidery;
cotton warp, wool weft; 30 by
66 in. Photo: Grant Kernan

*My experience is that the physi-
cal realities of a country pro-
foundly influence the psyche and
the culture of the people living
there. In this tapestry, I tried to
capture some of the contrasts I
enjoy in the aspen parklands of
the Canadian prairies, which are
a significant part of my identity.*

C

SUZANNE PRETTY
UNITED STATES

Fragmentation

Tapestry; linen warp, wool, silk,
cotton; 45 by 67 in.
Photo: Andy Edgar

*Contemporary society is break-
ing the natural environment into
small isolated pieces, fragmented
and separated by ribbons of
pavement and development.*

D

PAM PATRIE
UNITED STATES

View from My Day Job

Tapestry; cotton warp, wool weft;
48 by 60 in. Photo: Frank Engel

*I am torn after almost 20 years of
working as a bridge tender to
support my studio and its expen-
sive medium. Do I quit the job or
quit the weaving and paint in
another medium?*

A

B

C

D

A

B

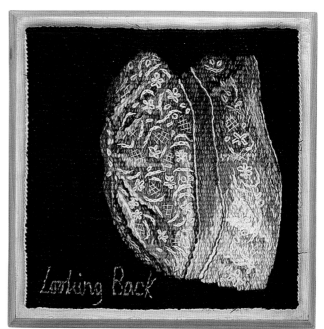

C

A

MARGO MACDONALD
UNITED STATES

Dark Lake Chair
Tapestry; cotton warp, wool
weft; 27 by 24 in.

B

VALERIE KIRK
AUSTRALIA

*Looking Forward—Looking
Back 2*
Tapestry; wool, cotton, linen; 3¼
by 3¼ in. Photo: Nancy
McCracken

C

CECILIA BLOMBERG
UNITED STATES

By Lake Mälaren
Flat tapestry; cotton seine twine
warp, wool weft; 37 by 43 in.

D

D

JANE KIDD
CANADA

Emblem/Endearment
(and detail)
Tapestry; wool, silk, rayon, cotton, metallic yarn; 36 by 36 in.
Photo: John Dean

E

E

ULRIKA LEANDER
UNITED STATES

Forbidden Fruit
Tapestry; cotton warp, wool weft; 49 by 50 in.
Photo: J. W. Nave

The inner gifts of love, joy, and passion lie waiting, untouched, sometimes forbidden.

A

TATYANA KHVTISIASHVILI
UNITED STATES

Farewell to Tbilisi

Tapestry; cotton warp, hand-dyed
wool weft; 28½ by 27½ in.

*Tbilisi is the beautiful capital of
the country of Georgia. Both are
a part of what I am and what my
tapestries are. The memories of
them are with me forever.*

B

JUDITH POXSON FAWKES
UNITED STATES

Curtained Cross Vaults

Inlay tapestry; linen; 72 by 70 in.
Photo: Bill Bachhuber

C

JAY WILSON
UNITED STATES

Through a Looking Glass

Tapestry; linen warp, commercial,
hand spun, and vegetal-dyed
wool weft; 79 by 48 in. Photo:
Paul Kodama, collection of State
Foundation on Culture and the
Arts, Hawaii

D

ION GRIGORE
ROMANIA

Village

Aubusson tapestry; wool; 70 by
33 in

E

ALISON KEENAN
CANADA

Morning Light

Gobelin tapestry; wool, cotton,
silk; 36 by 48 in. Photo: Robyn
Laba

*I am exploring the architectural
construction of an old city, both
abstract and real, as well as the
color transitions creating light
and shadow. Old life, and new
life protected and honored, are
the diverse images that reflect my
concern for the environment,
especially global warming.*

A

B

C

D

E

A

IEVA KRUMINA
LATVIA

The Moon Boat I and II
Tapestry, mixed techniques; wool,
linen; each 98¼ by 33½ in.

B

ANN SCHUMACHER
UNITED STATES

Inner Spaces
Tapestry; silk, linen, hand-dyed
wool; 31 by 52 in. Photo: M.S.
Rezny

*One goes to the inner spaces of
the mind when it is time to create, time to reflect, time to be....*

A

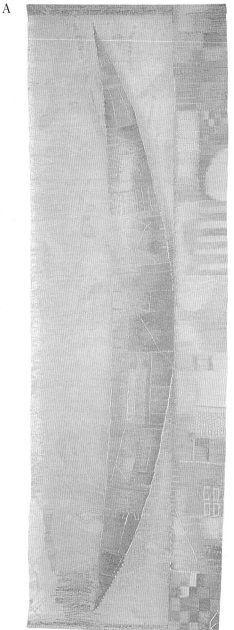
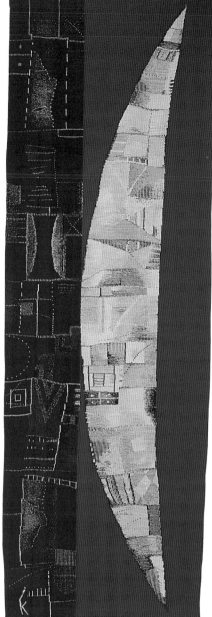

B

C

D

E

C

MINA LEVITAN-BABENSKIENE
LITHUANIA

Blue Space
Tapestry; linen, wool, silk, lurex;
37½ by 47 in.

D

MAIA TSINAMDZQVR-
ISHVILI
REPUBLIC OF GEORGIA

Summertime
Tapestry; wool; 31½ by 35 in.

E

MARIA LUISA FERREIRA
PORTUGAL

Radiance
Tapestry; linen, cotton, silk;
62 by 62 in.
Photo: Antonio Mil-Homens

A

SARAH SWETT
UNITED STATES

Hands

Tapestry, knitting; handspun silk
and wool, natural dye; 24 by 21
by 3 in. Photo: Mark La Moreaux

B

CECILIA BLOMBERG
UNITED STATES

Waiting by Tullgarn Castle

Flat tapestry, brocade; cotton
seine twine warp, wool weft; 24
by 48 in.

*I'm drawn to the Swedish land-
scape, probably out of nostalgia
and a bit of homesickness.*

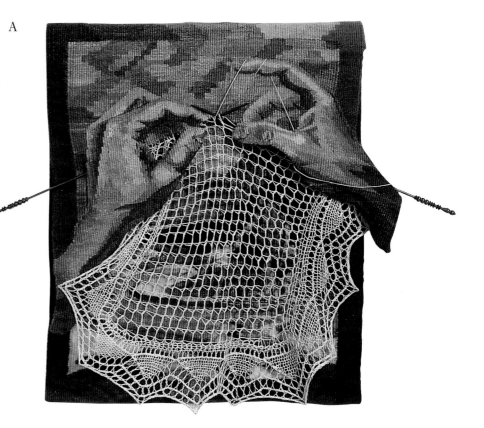

B

C

NANCY JACKSON
UNITED STATES

Trev's Blues I/III
Gobeln/Aubusson tapestry; cotton warp, wool and silk weft; 36 by 48 in.

D

ANN BADDELEY KEISTER
UNITED STATES

Leaving Home
Tapestry; wool; 51 by 57 in.
Photo: David Keister

D

JOLIE BIRD
CANADA

Lil Puddin'
Shaped tapestry; cotton, wool,
acrylic; 60 by 40 in.
Photo: Josie Chu

My work has been heavily influenced by popular culture but, in this instance, I have created a pop image instead of borrowing it.

ARTISTS' INDEX

AUDREY MOORE

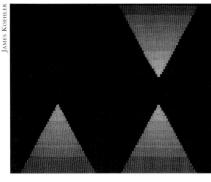

JAMES KOEHLER

HELGA BERRY

SUSAN WEBB LEE

PATTY HAWKINS

SALLY BROADWELL

CAS HOLMES

DIANNE SHULLENBERGER